Presented To:

_____

From:

_____

Date:

_____

THE
SHIFTING
ROMANCE
WITH
ISRAEL

THE
SHIFTING
ROMANCE
WITH
ISRAEL

American Pentecostal Ideology of
Zionism and the Jewish State

DR. RAYMOND L. GANNON

DESTINY IMAGE® PUBLISHERS, INC.

PO Box 310, Shippensburg, PA 17257-0310

"Promoting Inspired Lives."

This book and all other Destiny Image, Revival Press, MercyPlace, Fresh Bread, Destiny Image Fiction, and Treasure House books are available at Christian bookstores and distributors worldwide.

For a U.S. bookstore nearest you, call **1-800-722-6774**.

For more information on foreign distributors, call **717-532-3040**.

Reach us on the Internet: **www.destinyimage.com.**

Trade Paper: 978-0-7684-4109-3

Ebook: 978-0-7684-8857-9

For Worldwide Distribution, Printed in the U.S.A.

1 2 3 4 5 6 / 14 13 12

DEDICATION

I dedicate this volume to all those Spirit-filled Believers who are intent on bringing Yeshua's message of salvation and the Messianic Kingdom of God to "All Israel" in this generation.

ACKNOWLEDGMENTS

There are many who helped me along the way with my extensive research for the preparation of first the dissertation and now the book, *The Shifting Romance With Israel*.

When I had presumed my pursuit of education had finally reached its high point by the mid-1980s, Moishe Rosen, founder of Jews for Jesus, strongly encouraged me to pursue a second Ph.D. at either Oxford or Cambridge. Although I ultimately opted to do the Ph.D. at the Hebrew University of Jerusalem, it was Moishe's strong push and certainty of the Messianic Movement's need that I do this that compelled me to consider another research degree.

On the 75th anniversary of the Balfour Declaration, November 17, 1992, as a resident of Jerusalem, I found myself sitting in the sun next to a man I had been hoping to meet for some months due to his vast research on Christian Zionism and Jewish Missions. While we awaited the commencement of celebrations at Christ Church inside Old Jerusalem's Jaffa Gate, I told Dr. Yaakov Ariel, professor at the Hebrew University of Jerusalem, that I was intending to research the American Evangelical and Pentecostal growing ambivalence toward national Israel. He then invited me to consider doing the Ph.D. on this research topic at the Hebrew University. He later served as one of the official readers for the dissertation from his new post at the University of North Carolina.

Dr. Yaakov Ariel soon introduced me to Professor Avihu Zakai, an Israeli world-class religious historian with keen areas of specialization on Anglo-American Puritans and Jonathan Edwards in particular. I was deeply gratified by Professor Zakai's willingness to serve as my mentor for the Ph.D. His great efforts to supervise my work over long years ultimately yielded the Summa Cum Laude distinction for the dissertation as awarded by the Senate of the Hebrew University of Jerusalem in 2004. Avihu Zakai has strongly pushed me since 2003 to publish *The Shifting Romance With Israel*.

I am also indebted for multiplied forms of assistance along the way to ultimate publication. At the invitation of Dr. Gerald Anderson, my family members were guest residents at the Overseas Missions Study Center in New Haven, Connecticut, in 1993-1994. I was then privileged to commence my research at The Day Missions Library within the Yale Divinity School Library.

I did much of my preliminary collecting of vital research materials at Lee University (Church of God) in Cleveland, Tennessee. Dr. David Roebuck, Director of the Dixon Pentecostal Research Center (Church of God) and later long-term executive director for the Society for Pentecostal Studies, was immensely helpful in providing me assistance in rapidly locating and copying materials I would need for my historical investigation.

Much gratitude is owed as well to Dr. Joseph Marics of the Assemblies of God Theological Seminary (AGTS) who facilitated the use of archived materials in Springfield, Missouri. The Assemblies of God were the first of the major Pentecostal fellowships to collect vast reservoirs of archived materials that would prove so vital to my work. The chief location for these collections is the Flower Pentecostal Heritage Center in Springfield, Missouri. Wayne Warner, the immediate past director, Joyce Lee, archivist, and Glenn Gohr, assistant archivist, were all superbly helpful in enabling me to access the treasure trove of collected materials that covered most of the 20th century.

Friends at Oral Roberts University likewise proved to be immensely useful for my investigation. Special thanks to Dr. Vinson Synan who oversaw the creation of the archives at the Oral Roberts University Holy Spirit Research Center and to James Zeigler who graciously supported my labors there with both his encouragement and expertise. Time spent there with Dr. Brad Young was highly useful as he provided both inspiration and direction for the project.

Dr. Russell Spittler, at that time director of the David DuPlessis Archive at Fuller Theological Seminary, was very encouraging of the project and was pleased to make archival materials available to me. Dr. Cecil "Mel" Robeck, a friend from our student days at Bethany Bible College in the late 1960s and current director of the David DuPlessis Archive and professor of Church History and Ecumenics at Fuller Theological Seminary, made his private collection of Pentecostal research available to me. I discovered valuable pieces to important puzzles in his office in Pasadena.

Jews for Jesus, under the direction of Moishe Rosen, opened their Hospitality House to me for some weeks while I plumbed the depths of their research collections and library under the direction of Dr. Rich Robinson, their resident scholar. Dr. Robinson was always helpful and encouraging along the way as is his constant manner.

Of course, I was also privileged to access the library at my old alma mater, Princeton Theological Seminary, where new historical treasures were located, as well as at the vast religious history collections at the Hebrew University of Jerusalem, where my family and I lived for many years.

There are numerous others to whom I am deeply grateful for all their helps and encouragement provided along the way. Dr. Del Tarr, immediate past president of the Assemblies of God Theological Seminary (AGTS) in Springfield, Missouri, invited me to teach at AGTS during lengthy portions of each academic year from 1996-2000 where I could continue to work on *The Shifting Romance With Israel*. George Geesey, my part-time student secretary, labored long hours entering data into my research banks. Outstanding world missions personnel, Drs. Paul and Wardine Wood were both extremely anxious for me to finish the research and degree. I found all their "pushing" very rewarding.

Dr. Lois E. Olena, current director of the Society for Pentecostal Studies, served with our larger Israel's Redemption ministry team prior to her moving to faculty status at AGTS. Dr. Olena's tireless efforts at proofreading and editing the Ph.D. dissertation, both before and after official submission, contributed much to the expertise of the text.

Assemblies of God grand patriarch, Dr. Stanley M. Horton is a hero of the faith by any standard. Dr. Horton's academic and theological contributions to the Assemblies of God, the best archived of all the larger Pentecostal groups, has been immensely important to Pentecostals of all national, cultural, and ethnic stripes across the world for 60 years. His perpetual devotion to the Pentecostal cause combined with his clear vision for the "salvation of All Israel," lent great strength to the tremendous inspiration he has afforded me in this effort. I am thankful, too, to Dean Drawbaugh of Destiny Image. His readiness to publish a popularized version of my academic research at the Hebrew University of Jerusalem is deeply prized. I am so pleased to realize that Destiny Image has now opened a Messianic label for this very kind of publication.

And finally, I must acknowledge the many years of sacrifice my wife, Kassiani, has endured patiently awaiting the concluding hours on first the dissertation and now its popularized version. No words can describe my sense of gratitude for her being alongside me in all our joint efforts now well into five decades. She has always proven to be a phenomenal source of spiritual renewal even while quietly suffering her fate as my non-stop team player. To Kassiani, apart from my salvation, I owe all things.

CONTENTS

FOREWORD

Is anti-Semitism on the rise? If we look at what the major denominations are doing, it surely seems so. Their bureaucracies make statements that are both anti-American and anti-Israel. They are promoting a serious "anti-Israel bandwagon," divesting their investments in any company doing business in Israel.[1] They ignore the sad fact that the prevention of terror "is an enormous burden on Israel."[2] Worse, they reject plain statements in Bible prophecy that show God still has a plan for national Israel and its people.

Unfortunately, it is not only the theological liberals who are disregarding or explaining away Bible prophecy concerning Israel. Many who claim to be conservative, Bible-believing people have adopted a replacement theology that says all those prophecies must be modified and applied to the Church, leaving no place for Israel in God's future dealings with the world. To them, the nation of Israel and the Jews have no place in God's plan.

The question arises then, "Where do Pentecostals stand in this controversy?" Dr. Raymond L. Gannon has the experience and insight to give us the answer. His Ph.D. dissertation submitted to and accepted by the Hebrew University of Jerusalem gives us a clear picture of *"The Shifting Romance with Israel"* as seen in "American Pentecostal Theology of Zionism and the Jewish State" over the course of the last century. He lets us see the difficulties and the hope.

Raymond Gannon has been intimately involved in Pentecostal relationships with the Jews and Israel. The Assemblies of God have chosen him as their national representative for Jewish ministries and as their ambassador to "All Israel." Among his accomplishments are two doctorates and four master's degrees. His many published articles show the breadth of his understanding of the needs and methods of ministry to the Jews and Israel. He has served as pastor of three Messianic congregations and as a professor of missions and Jewish studies in colleges and universities in Israel and America. He founded the Israel College of the Bible with campuses in Jerusalem, Haifa, and Tel Aviv, with classes in four languages: Hebrew, English, Russian, and Amharic (Ethiopian). He spearheaded Russian Jewish and Ethiopian ministries in Israel.

Pentecostal believers, leaders, pastors, and teachers will find warnings of dangers to Pentecostal theology of Israel in this volume. We will also find encouragement and new hope for Israel today. As Pentecostals we need to "reinforce Israel's abiding significance to God and, certainly, to Pentecostalism." Raymond Gannon and his writings will help us.

STANLEY M. HORTON,
Th.D., Distinguished Professor Emeritus of Bible and Theology,
Assemblies of God Theological Seminary,
Springfield, Missouri

PREFACE

As a youth of nearly 14 years, I came into a rich Pentecostal experience and heritage. My paternal grandparents were Assemblies of God ministers of the old "Pentecostal bun" generation. In 1962, I not only found Jesus but felt the call of God upon my life to proclaim the Gospel to "All Israel."

I found enthusiastic support among the Pentecostals of my parents' generation who could remember the reestablishment of the Jewish State of Israel in 1948 arising out of the ashes of the Shoah or Holocaust. It seemed that everyone in our Pentecostal circle took the gathering of the Jewish people to Zion as clear prophetic evidence that the Second Coming was at hand.

The summer Kassiani and I married saw the apocalyptic events of the 1967 Six Day War in which Old Jerusalem, including the Temple Mount, was retaken by Israeli forces after a two millennia hiatus. No longer in non-Jewish hands, the resumption of Jewish life in a free Jerusalem suggested "the times of the Gentiles" were nearing their end. Soon the King of Israel, the Jewish Messiah Jesus, would return to Jerusalem and take His kingly throne in Zion. Bible-believing Christians of all stripes thrilled to the realization that the "last days" were upon us.

Failing to get to Israel upon Bible college graduation in 1970, Kassiani and I moved to Los Angeles. In the same year we pioneered a Spirit-filled

Messianic Synagogue, the 1973 Yom Kippur War raged in the Middle East. In distinction to the Six Day War, Israel now suffered profound losses before ultimately coming to a truce with her enemies. This represented no small shock to Evangelical and Pentecostal Christians who were predisposed by their dispensationalist theology and recent history to expect nothing but victory in Israel's camp.

At the same time, oil crises began plaguing the West as oil-producing Arab states determined to punish the West for its support of Israel. The media onslaught decrying Israel's troubled relations to angry and dangerously armed Muslim militias, like Yasser Arafat's Palestine Liberation Organization, made Israel the culprit.

Christians, both Evangelicals and Pentecostal, were increasingly influenced by oil shortages and negative media portrayal more than they were informed by the biblical promises to Israel. In time, as tracked here in *The Shifting Romance With Israel,* stalwart Christian supporters of the Zionist enterprise began to have misgivings. Three generations of Evangelicals and Pentecostals had favorably looked upon Zion. But now in the mid-1970s, there were signs of deterioration in the traditional relationship.

As one fully engaged in proclaiming the Gospel to "All Israel," I deeply felt the growing coldness of my Christian fellows toward the Zionist state. Denominational periodicals, once valiantly proclaiming their enthusiasm for the infrastructural developments in Haifa and Tel Aviv, were now stone cold toward the State of Israel. They offered no support or credibility to the very existence of the Jewish State or its defense apart from its eventual survival in the utopian future.

I watched this grow even more tellingly in the 1980s in my own denomination, the Assemblies of God. Decreasing confidence in Israel's immediate future was evident by the deliberate silence of church officialdom who had resolved to remove themselves from any accusation of being "pro-Jewish" or "Zionists."

Surely there were many factors in the Evangelical and Pentecostal official and very intentional chilling down of their own previously warm disposition toward the State of Israel. But while denominational magazines and teaching materials might still point out the value of touring the Land of the Bible, report on Bible distribution in Israel, or revel in new archaeological finds, nothing in support of the Jewish State could be found in some denominations' literature for the last quarter of the 20th century.

Because of my own Pentecostal heritage, biblical convictions, and professional relations with both the Christian and Jewish worlds, I grew increasingly frustrated. Was this chilled sentiment just my imagination? Or did a real cause or identifiable causes exist for purposeful Christian disassociation from the Zionist dream? I did not have simplistic answers like "Christians are anti-Semitic," or "the Church is backslidden." I knew Evangelicals and Pentecostals loved Jewish people and remained committed to Jewish evangelism. But why the not-so-subtle disconnect with the Jewish State?

I decided to make a serious study of this issue by the early 1990s. And, as fate would have it, a door opened for me to research my question as a Ph.D. dissertation at the Hebrew University of Jerusalem. Returning to the United States in 1993 for a furlough, I began my investigation. I intended first to study the growing Christian denominational distancing from Israel in the wing of the Church known as Evangelicalism and Pentecostalism. But I soon discovered this was too vast a range of Christians for the strictures of one doctoral dissertation. So I resolved to limit my research investigation to the Pentecostal world. But I was soon disappointed to discover that Pentecostals had only within more recent years begun to collect archival materials. They had collected so very little in the way of archived materials that I would never be able to draw sound academic conclusions on the basis of so little evidence.

I was very gratified, however, to discover that my own denomination, the Assemblies of God, had been devoted for many years to the accumulation of literatures, relics, teaching materials, periodicals, missions records, etc., that covered most of the 20th century, the Pentecostal century. So, not by choice but of necessity, I was compelled to examine *The Shifting Romance With Israel* within the Assemblies of God.

While this study focuses in particular upon Assemblies of God Pentecostalism, it nevertheless reflects the larger Evangelical and Pentecostal drifting away from a formerly strong bond to Zionism and the Jewish state. This book then will be useful to all Evangelicals and Pentecostals who want to answer the same nagging question as to why their own denominations or church fellowships have stepped back from their earlier love affair with Israel.

I first trace the sources for early 20th century Christian thinking as they relate to the future of national Israel as discovered in 17th-century Puritanism, 18th -entury Post-Millennialism, and finally 19th-century dispensationalism. Then the 20th century is historically partitioned to examine the issues that produced years of rather dramatic changes. The Pentecostal romance with Israel ran hot and cold, up and down, in and out, over the full 20th century. This book traces that "shifting romance" and draws conclusions that might surprise you.

I hope you enjoy your read.

Raymond L. Gannon, Ph.D.
December 4, 2011

INTRODUCTION

The beginning of the 20th century witnessed the nativity of fraternal twin movements: Zionism and American Pentecostalism. Both newborns, initially treated as weak and infantile in a religiously hostile world, had a basis of ideological support in three centuries of American myth and motif.

The burgeoning Pentecostal movement of the early decades of the twentieth-century, with its chief distinctive of speaking in tongues as initial evidence of Spirit-baptism, had great difficulty persuading Christian contemporaries of the biblical legitimacy of their unique doctrine or of their justification for Pentecostal group existence on either historical or theological grounds. To assure the perpetuity of the Pentecostal movement, a "Latter Rain" ideology centering around Hebrew prophecies of the Spirit's outpouring in the "last days" was quickly fashioned. This "Latter Rain" ideology used the contemporary Zionist revival as corroborating evidence of the associated divine undertakings to restore both Israel and the Church to their respective proper places in keeping with the divine strategy for the endtimes. Israel was to be restored to Zion even as the Church was to be restored to its radical first-century apostolic essence.

These divinely initiated twin restorationist efforts would bring Israel and the Church back full cycle to their 1st-century points of departure as an immediate prelude to the culmination of salvation history.

My research analyzes the one-sided and shifting romance of American Pentecostalism with Zionism and the Jewish State from the birth of the Pentecostal movement in 1901 until the end of the 20ᵗʰ century.

Past historical scholarship has carefully considered the different ideologies of Roman Catholicism and Protestantism as they touched upon the question of Israel's role in the *eschaton* (the "last days of time" or "the end of the age"). Thorough analyses, too, have been made of the Evangelical and Fundamentalist Christian devotion to the Zionist enterprise in light of their eschatological perspective on the Second Coming.

But my research, revealed within these pages, is the first to analyze the century-long intellectual history of American Pentecostalism over several periods of romantically shifting sentiment on Zionism and the Jewish State as Pentecostal ideology has been impacted by political, social, economic, and missiological developments.

GOD'S NEW ISRAEL

The American Puritans had come to the New World ostensibly to function as God's "New Israel." However, this Puritan outlook did not preclude for them the importance of a nationally restored Israel in the eschaton. Some Puritan writers concurrently anticipated a new Pentecost to be outpoured upon the spiritually revived Church to affect both increased sanctity and divine empowerment for Gospel global conquest.

God's chosen American had experienced spiritual phenomena during the Great Awakening and related American revivals of the 18th century ostensibly as a means to intensified piety and power. But Jonathan Edwards' postmillennialism had only envisioned a restored Jewish State at the climax of a thousand-year march to the Christian redemption of the world. The 19th century's newly introduced theological scheme of dispensationalism ideologically afforded a revitalized Jewish State a crucial role in a future utopian millennial age Kingdom of God. This multifaceted New World heritage predisposed American Pentecostalism to eagerly salute the rising banner of Zionism particularly since Pentecostals viewed themselves as playing their own vital role in the "last days" or eschaton. A nationally restored Israel and a spiritually restored Church were to fully partner in the closing days of salvation history.

As the initial Pentecostal Latter Rain movement gained ideological momentum over its first generation to the end of World War I, its disposition toward Zionism soared according to the dramatically sequenced events of the war—the Balfour Declaration (the British statement that favored a Jewish homeland being established in Palestine), General Allenby's capture of Jerusalem, and the preliminary infrastructural developments in Zion. British political backpedaling combined with rising Western anti-Semitism to both anger and frighten Pentecostals. Over time, some began to question the inevitability of Zionism's success since Israel had yet to come to faith in Christ. While reaction against anti-Semitism stiffened in Pentecostal circles in the 1930s and 1940s, and enthusiasm for a Jewish State persisted, so did continued pockets of Pentecostal doubt.

After World War II, Pentecostals could pride themselves in their new levels of social acceptance in the Evangelical world and wanted nothing to jeopardize their new status. In part to allow for the potential demise of the infant Jewish State within Pentecostal ideology, the Assemblies of God, the leading Pentecostal denomination, found itself prepared to move away from its Latter Rain moorings in favor of a dispensationalist perspective which theologically shunted Israel's divinely promised destiny off into an uncertain eschatological and utopian future.

The years of international threat against Israel immediately preceding the wars of 1948-49, 1956, 1967, and 1973, found Pentecostals dramatically stepping back from strong identification with an Israel in jeopardy.

But the glorious Israeli victories in 1949, 1956, and 1967 resulted in temporary Pentecostal euphoria and celebration of the pending restorationist climax of the ages. The Yom Kippur War of 1973, however, was a watershed event that motivated the Assemblies of God to organizationally fully disassociate from the Zionist enterprise for political, economic, and missiological causes.

Only within the final two decades of the 20th century were there renewed calls to a certain sense of eschatological partnership with Israel in Pentecostal ideology, as it had been recognized that the classical Pentecostal distinctive and very reason for Pentecostal organizational existence are inseparably bound to the success of the Jewish State.

Chapter 1

THE HISTORICAL SOURCES FOR THE PENTECOSTAL IDEOLOGY OF ISRAEL

For I do not want you, brothers, to be ignorant of this mystery—lest you be wise in your own eyes—that a partial hardening has come upon Israel until the fullness of the Gentiles has come in; and in this way all Israel will be saved, as it is written, "The Deliverer shall come out of Zion. He shall turn away ungodliness from Jacob" (Romans 11:25-26 Tree of Life Bible).

What are the historical founts that informed American Pentecostalism's ideas and beliefs concerning Israel? It will help us to understand the Pentecostal ideology of Zionism and the Jewish State if we track the impactful history of the first three centuries of American classical views of the biblically promised spiritual transformation and national restoration of Israel. These main classical sources include 17th-century Puritan historical premillennialism. 18th-century New Light postmillennialism, and 19th-century Holiness and dispensationalist schools.

PURITAN IDEOLOGY OF ISRAEL

New World Puritans related themselves to both biblical and eschatological Israel. This fraternal identification helped foster an American cultural empathy with the Jewish People. This sense of affinity with Israel was passed on like a baton to succeeding generations.

Puritans laid the foundation for American revivalist thought concerning the future role of the Chosen People. The Puritans were devoted to the spiritual restoration of first-century Christianity. They were literalists in their interpretation of the Bible, and their worldview included a Providence active in space and time. Their aspiration toward the spiritual restoration of the Church to its first-century Book of Acts sanctity coupled with their conviction of God's activity in the real world led them to anticipate an active partnership with the Chosen People in salvation history and Israel's national restoration. They expected to be conjoined with the apostle Paul's *"all Israel"* of Romans 11:26 in the victorious divine summation of human history.

Key Protestant reformers had regarded the Book of Revelation as the authoritative guide to both human and salvation history. Neither Martin Luther nor John Calvin foresaw in Scripture the spiritual transformation of national Israel resulting from Jewish faith in Christ. Yet, Martin Bucer at Cambridge and Peter Martyr at Oxford did see a future calling of Israel in the Bible. In 1560, the Geneva Bible included a marginal reading at Romans 11:25-26, "He sheweth that the time shall come that the whole nation of the Jews, though not every one particularly, shall be joined to the Church of Christ."

British Protestant John Foxe (1516–1587) had suggested in 1563 that England was the elect nation. In contrast to other Puritan writers, he saw no unique role for "all Israel" other than what occurred in centuries past.[1] English Puritans originally embraced the idea that England was the Promised Land and the British the Chosen People. It was they who would usher in the millennial age.

Puritans with an Augustinian theology believed Romans 11:25-26 referred to a spiritual rather than a national restoration of Israel. Others saw final reconciliation of God and Israel in Christ only in terms of bringing blessing to all nations, in a worldwide Kingdom of God.

By mid-17th century, Reformed theology had embraced belief in a Second Coming preceded by the salvation of national Israel. Puritans advocating a coming millennial kingdom envisioned the Jewish return to Israel's Messiah Jesus as the first major millennial event. However, they still hoped that British people and their king would awaken to do God's work. But when Oliver Cromwell (1599–1658) was deposed, that hope quickly dissipated.

Increasing numbers of British Puritans felt compelled to go to the New World. They expected that there God would set His Puritan saints free to build "a city upon a hill" to correspond to the New Jerusalem. Puritans longed to be able to practice New Testament faith and wholeheartedly worship free of the religious hegemony they suffered in England.

PURITAN PURSUIT OF RESTORATION AND ISRAEL

The Puritan objective was a fully restored apostolic Church that would enlighten the nations, foster universal faith in Christ, and inspire the redemption of national Israel. While Catholics and Anglicans would appeal to church history and traditions, Puritans bypassed both history and tradition in their desire to go back to the order of things as seen in the Book of Acts. Like their Pentecostal heirs, Puritans could not find cooperation from either the Church establishment or society, so they turned their backs on both.

Puritans envisioned three stages of church history. Stage one was from the early church to Constantine, from the Book of Acts to the Roman embrace of Christianity. Stage two was the era of church decline and apostasy, from the fourth century to the Reformation. Stage three began with the Reformation and was now continuing toward an earthly climax. American Puritan New

Israel, like Israel of old, considered themselves delivered out of bondage, carried through the sea, and now commissioned to complete the stalled work of the Reformation.[2]

Massachusetts Bay Colony Puritan pastor John Cotton (1584–1652) was first introduced to Puritanism when studying at the University of Cambridge in England. He was interested in the spiritual restoration of the Church to its point of origin but did not associate this with a millennial or "end-time" fulfillment. Puritan millennialism, however, represented the zenith of the Church's restorationist hope. The spiritual unity of the New Covenant peoples, Israel and the Church, was perceived as vital to genuinely God-honoring restoration. Puritan millennialism was linked to such partnership goals, since the divinely produced restoration would find its fulfillment in the final reversion to the original God-intended conditions for both Israel and the Church, as those united in a New Covenant working relationship.

When English authorities filed charges against Cotton for religious nonconformity, he sailed to the New World and became an influential leader in the Massachusetts Bay Colony, the new center for the fulfillment of salvation history. New England functioned as the New Israel. Its communal submission to Christ would ultimately generate a double-edged witness to the nations: (1) the establishment of a God-centered model nation to demonstrate the wisdom and value of national submission to God, and (2) the primary Christian mission agency to impact all humankind with the Gospel and prepare the nations to give allegiance to Christ.

Roger Williams, English clergyman, American colonist, and founder of Rhode Island, believed that the Christian task now was to denounce religious error and to wait for God's impending restoration of "lost Zion."[3] Christianity could only be restored as the New Testament Church was revitalized. He claimed, "The New Testament alone is the 'true patterne' for the life of God's people."[4] Visible signs as in the Book of Acts were manifestations of God's presence. The Spirit would pour forth again fiery streams of tongues and prophecy. Only God could recreate His Church into its spiritually pristine condition that would climax in the Second Coming.

PURITAN LITERALISM IN BIBLICAL INTERPRETATION AND ISRAEL

Hebraic studies profoundly influenced Puritan thought. Though Jewish people were few in the New World, the Hebrew Bible and rabbinic Judaism were significant American realities. Enthusiasm for Hebraic studies saw Hebrew as useful for Christology. In addition, the Hebrew Bible afforded a model for divinely established theocracy. Rabbinical literature suggested a literal restoration of the Jewish people to Zion consistent with Romans 11:26, "all Israel shall be saved."

Some argued against Jewish restoration and wanted to only spiritualize the prophecies. But growing interest in Hebraic studies helped foster rabbinic pollination of Christian apocalypticism. Hugh Broughton (1549–1612), Jewish missionary in the Levant, proposed translating the New Testament to Hebrew for Jewish consumption. His *Commentary on Daniel*, published in 1596, inspired further investigation into the question of Jewish national spiritual transformation.

Protestant reformers reintroduced the concept of divine impact upon history. This provided new meaning to eschatology and the millennium, giving new significance to the Jewish people in Puritan thought. Paul's "all Israel" would embrace Christ. Prophecy teachers advocated that sometime during a second millennium (a.d. 1300–2300), a great battle would take place between the Turks and their allies and a restored Jewish nation in Zion. God would intervene to miraculously rescue His people. A rebuilt Jerusalem would become the international center of godliness, true religion, and a faithful universe. Then the Second Coming with the resurrections of saints and sinners to universal judgment would be experienced in space and time.

The extremist "Fifth Monarchy" faction believed they were divinely called to establish a New Jerusalem. They were fascinated with the prospect of apocalyptic Jewish spiritual transformation and national return to Zion. But the Puritans saw no purpose for sending missionaries to the Jewish people until the "great Whore, the city of Rome" was destroyed.[5]

By the third and fourth generation of American Puritanism, Puritans were anticipating a literal millennial reign of Jesus from Zion. Divinely orchestrated change from the present age to the millennial age would be essential for the Church to be restored to its original New Testament pattern: "The millennium became a way to hope for the restoration of the past by transposing it into the time to come."[6]

17TH CENTURY PURITAN MILLENNIALISM AND A CLOUD OF WITNESSES TO ESCHATOLOGICAL ISRAEL

Puritan theologians did much to influence English thinking as well as those English emigrants who journeyed to the New World seeking religious freedom. Thomas Brightman (1562–1607), an English clergyman known for his exegesis of the Book of Revelation, emphasized both the spiritual restoration of Israel and a millennium in which the Kingdom of God could be fully operational on earth within a generation. However, two questions remained: (1) Would Israel be restored in Zion, and, if so, would it occur prior to, simultaneously with, or after the Second Coming? And (2) To what extent would Israel's restoration be connected to the Church's spiritual revitalization? Would miracles and speaking in tongues in the Church accompany a spiritually revitalized Israel?

Brightman provided Puritans a sense of important personal involvement in the cataclysm between the powers of good and evil, between Christ and antichrist. Rather than putting their hopes in fallible princes, he advocated advancing the Reformation cause. Proactive engagement on earth could bring fulfillment of prophecies of the Book of Revelation within their own lifetimes.

Brightman assigned the sixth vial of the Book of Revelation (see Rev. 6:12) to the spiritual transformation of "all Israel" and as the immediate prelude to the millennium. Jerusalem would be wholly restored. The Jewish people would embrace Jesus as Israel's King-Messiah, and the earth would be "filled with the knowledge of the Lord" (see Hab. 2:14).

Brightman influenced Puritan and American theology for centuries. His eight reasons why Christians should evangelize the Jewish people included the biblical tenet that God's covenant with Abraham would never be cancelled. He saw Ezekiel's vision of the dry bones (see Ezek. 37) as the basis for Jewish spiritual transformation to Christ and the restoration of the Twelve Tribes.

Many regard German-born Johann Alsted (1588–1638) as a father to modern premillennialism. He used Jewish apocalyptic literature in his *The Beloved City* (1643) to show the Jewish people would be delivered from the antichrist and as a nation come to faith in Jesus during the millennium. Joseph Mede's (1586–1638) *Clavis Apocalyptica* (1627) also promoted premillennialism using rabbinical writings. Mede equated the seventh millennium with Judgment Day in his *Key to the Revelation* (1643). It would begin with resurrection of the faithful and end with resurrection of the wicked. The Jewish people would, like Paul, have their Damascus Road experience and become obedient to Christ. They would provide astonishing international witness leading to the spiritual transformation of the last Gentile holdouts.

Mede connected Puritan ideas of national Jewish spiritual transformation with revitalized Church expansion. Christ's reign on earth would establish a new world order. The Church would experience a new outpouring of the Holy Spirit replete with the gifts of the Spirit (see Joel 2:28-32; 1 Cor. 13; Rom. 12). Mede's writings thrust the millennium into the fore of Puritan thought.

Mentioned previously, John Cotton anticipated a brief return of Christ to render judgment on humankind. Cotton preferred a return to early Christianity and the gradual development of God's earthly Kingdom. The lowest members of Jewish society would turn to Christ and gradually upper-class Jewish people would come to Him. For Cotton, New England would be the site for the fulfillment of biblical prophecies concerning Israel.

Sir Henry Finch's *The Calling of the Jews* (1621), was the first book to make the spiritual transformation of "all Israel" its chief theme. The Jewish believing community would be doctrinally pure. Happy and prosperous, the Promised Land would be fully populated and fertile. Jewish faith in the Messiah Jesus would encourage all nations to turn to Jesus and honor Israel. Because King James imagined the book advocated royal subservience to Jewish overlords, he arrested Finch and his publisher, but later released them. King James could not limit Finch's effectiveness as the first English advocate of a literal Jewish return to Zion.

In *The Day Breaking* (1647), American Thomas Shepard asked which might come first, the spiritual transformation of Israel or the universal ingathering of the Gentile nations. This was a contemporary concern since American Indian resistance to the Gospel was attributed to (1) the need for the Jewish people to come to Messianic faith first, (2) the need for Indians to be civilized, and (3) the need for restored first-century miracles and speaking in tongues. Note this linkage between Israel's spiritual transformation and restoration of New Testament Holy Spirit manifestations.

British cleric John Owen (1616–1683) preached to the House of Commons in 1652 that Revelation's sixth vial called for the Jewish people to come to faith in Jesus and be part of the Church. He did not anticipate a physical return of Israel to Zion or of Christ to reign on earth.

Increase Mather (1639–1723), however, did expect the Jewish people to return to Zion after coming to Christ as depicted in his book, *The Mystery of Israel's Salvation Explained and Applyed* (1669). Focusing on Romans 11:25-26, he insisted that literal interpretation was always to be preferred to allegorizing or spiritualizing. The Jewish people would possess the Promised Land.

Israel would not replace the Church in God's economy. Redeemed Israel would become "burning and shining lights" to the Gentile nations. The return from Babylonian captivity would pale in comparison to the Jewish return to Zion at Christ's Second Coming.

Mather believed that consistent with apostolic doctrine, spiritually redeemed Israel would be the "most glorious Nation" on earth.[7] All nations would hold Israel in high esteem, as Jewish people would be party to the blossoming of the desert. By 1710, he responded to reports of Jewish people coming to faith in Jesus in Europe as a foreglimpse of the religious revival that would lead to the Second Coming and the millennium.

Samuel Sewell (1652–1730) wrote in his *Phaenomena* (1697) that America could become "the seat of the Divine Metropolis" during the millennium. Light bearing Jewish people would "be entrusted with great Empire, and Rule in the World."[8] He believed the New Jerusalem would have a Jewish majority population, but hoped it would be in Mexico.

Cotton Mather (1663–1728), son of Increase Mather, prayed for the Jewish spiritual transformation to Christ. In 1690, he preached that Christian communities are to function as an "Israel of God." This was not replacement theology suggesting the Church's displacement of Israel as the "chosen people" as he still believed that Israel's best days were still ahead. The Second Coming would be signaled by collapse of the papacy, the end of Turkish hostilities, and most important, the dramatic growth of the international faith community as a result of Israel's spiritual transformation.

About 1715, millennial expectations were heightened by growing ecumenical unity between Christian groups and by Joseph Mede's proclamation that he calculated the Second Coming to be in 1716. William Whiston calculated the fall of the papacy (the antichrist) to be the same year. This, with reports of Jewish people turning to Christ in Western Europe, created immense eschatological tension for Mather. He believed Jesus would return literally and personally at His Second Coming. However, after the death of his father (1723), he spoke against the need to see the national spiritual transformation of Israel before the Second Coming. In 1724 he wrote that he was satisfied "that there is nothing to hinder the immediate Coming of our Saviour."[9] Later he revamped his earlier views and believed that the prophesied Jewish spiritual transformation probably occurred with the 1st-century Church and that contemporary Jewish national spiritual transformation was unlikely. His use of types also suggested that New England could not flatter herself into believing she had usurped all the scriptural promises to Israel.

18ᵀᴴ-CENTURY AMERICAN REVITALIZATION: REVIVAL AND REVOLUTION

The Pentecostal revival of the early 1900s was heir to both Jonathan Edwards' millennial ambitions and John Wesley's hunger for an encounter with the Spirit of sanctity. Though Pentecostals did not espouse Edwards' postmillennialism, they embraced his motif of global evangelism as America's mission and destiny. They viewed themselves as intended by God to ignite the fires of revival and spiritual renewal over the world as the prelude to the Second Coming.

Wesley's message of personal sanctification inspired them to expect a new encounter with God's Spirit so as to restore pristine New Testament Christianity. Along with this, a revitalized nation of Israel would reassert its prominence in a redeemed world.

Jonathan Edwards and the Great Awakening

Edwards exalted the current revival, later known as the Great Awakening, which he was sure was bringing a glorious transformation of the world into "Latter Day Glory," beginning in America. The new lights of the era, Jonathan Edwards and John Wesley, believed this revival was "the prelude" to the millennial Kingdom of God.[10] When revival fires cooled, Edwards no longer located the millennium in America. But he still held the postmillennial hope that progressively the forces of evil would eventually be defeated. Millennial bliss would be achieved prior to the Second Coming as the result of universal Gospel preaching.

John Wesley and the Rise of Methodism

John Wesley believed the revival of his day was a divine corrective to the traditionalist Church of England. A break with religious formalism was necessary for the genuine Gospel of grace to be released and to recover New Testament Christianity. The early Methodists relied on Scripture as the "sole rule of faith and practice."[11]

Wesley's restorationism directly affected the early Pentecostals. His advocacy of original, true Christianity was based on his conviction that Christianity of the first four centuries was the work of God Himself. He felt that after the Council of Nicea in A.D. 325, the Church became corrupted. But those under Methodist Holiness influence in later generations, like American Pentecostals, would freely bypass even early Christian centuries and go to the Book of Acts for a pattern to follow.[12]

Wesley was more interested in early Christian models for holy living than in the gifts of the Spirit. Yet he insisted that the spiritual gifts had continued in the early centuries. Only after the Council of Nicea did spiritual coldness and religious formality cause them to cease operating. He considered spiritual liberation as evidenced in demonstrative shouting, falling down, or "being slain by the Spirit" during public worship as a means to intensified spiritual assurance. As in later Pentecostalism, such assurance was expected as the work of the very present Spirit of God.[13]

The Wesleys and George Whitfield broke with tradition in many respects. They incorporated extemporaneous prayer, intimate group fellowship, the singing of freshly composed hymns with contemporary music, and mobile services. They, like later Pentecostals, abandoned religiously soured faces in favor of enthusiastic emphasis on the joys of Christian faith. Prayers directed to the Holy Spirit fostered expectation of spiritual fire. Yet the Holy Spirit's fuller coming for a grander possession of the believer was still anticipated. Thus, Methodism helped set the stage for Pentecostalism.

The Methodists saw themselves as a Hebraic-type redeemer nation in covenant relationship with God. They anticipated that God's Holy Spirit, whom they were experiencing, would soon sweep over the world. This understanding would profoundly impact Pentecostal expectations for both Israel and the Church.

John Fletcher, a protégé of Wesley, exalted the Day of Pentecost of Acts 2 to a defining event for the history of the Church, as significant as Christ's first coming. Pentecostals later used this emphasis in support of their emphasis on the Acts 2 experience of speaking in tongues in association with global evangelism and the Second Coming.[14]

THE BIBLICAL VISION OF ISRAEL AND THE NEW AMERICAN DREAM

The powerful sense of American mission and destiny first instilled by New England Puritans was reawakened by Jonathan Edwards and John Wesley.[15] After the French wars, preachers had referred to the English as "British Israel," suggesting the British were part of God's covenant people.[16]

Throughout the 18th century, premillennialist voices anticipated a Second Coming preceded by the consuming fire of God's judgment. Increase Mather also anticipated that the true Church, the Bride of Christ, would depart into the heavens to escape the fire and brimstone so deserved by the unfaithful. In 1727, Joseph Sewall preached that recent earthquakes were signs of the approaching Second Coming. All should be spiritually readied for widespread Gospel preaching, abundant outpouring of divine graces on the nations, and the salvation of all Israel that would herald an opening of heaven's blessings on all humankind, including New England.[17]

TRANSFORMATION OF
REVELATION TO REVOLUTION

The Great Awakening brought millennial expectations that fueled the demand for improved living circumstances that would benefit Americans first and the rest of the world second. It brought together American people of diversified ethnic and cultural backgrounds for the first time. George Whitfield's ecumenical style helped shape political unity. The spiritually revitalized American society shared common beliefs, standards, and attitudes. The Christian ethic of liberty transcended sectarianism.[18] The ideals of these 18th-century premillennialist voices supported the quest for nationhood in the American Revolution and laid the foundation for the "spirit of '76."[19]

In the 1750s, both pulpit and press called Americans back to Puritan motifs consistent with the providential election of the newly chosen American people. These motifs suggested a spiritually motivated continuation of the righteous cause of liberty—even to an increasingly secularized generation.

Using biblical imagery to support revolutionary ideas successfully combined the sacred and the secular. The grand divine design for America began with the "errand into the wilderness." It would soon lead into a divinely sponsored American Battle of Armageddon in which the British forces of evil would be deposed. The American Canaan would be transformed into the Promised Land of paradise and justice, a land flowing with milk and honey.[20]

Americans intuitively recognized the need for Christian pluralism. Denominational options had multiplied in the stir and aftermath of the Great Awakening. Yet the overarching support of Christian religion was seen as the cornerstone for the civic spirit of America. This instilled capacity for religious pluralism would characterize both the early Pentecostals and later

Charismatics in the 20th century. Both wanted to see the flow of spiritual gifts in all denominations.

The 1765 Stamp Act politicized Puritan millennial history. Even before that, a new millennialism perceived freedom as God's own cause for humankind. Puritan motif was now explained in terms of political development rather than mere piety.[21] The hope of global conversion to Christianity became combined with Christian commitment to America as the seat of liberty.[22]

In the latter half of the 18th century, the influence of Christian religion seemed to be weakening. Yet American conviction of the New World as the "Promised Land" only intensified. Biblical language disguised much of the natural instincts of politically oppressed Americans for vastly improved life on earth. Pulpit and press ably identified the political will of defiant Americans with the divine will for God's New Israel and the world. A redeemed New England would enthrone Christ in the latter days—from there He would govern the universe.[23]

Some new lights, like Joseph Bellamy (1719–1790), in his 1758 sermon "The Millennium," put the millennium into the distant future. This theoretically allowed divine intervention without a progressively improving world, a world that then continued to be filled with disappointment.

By 1760, the clergy blurred any demarcation between the interests of the Kingdom of God and American goals of political freedom. Civil and religious liberty became intertwined in clerical thought. The evil of tyranny in American thought surpassed even the dread of heresy. The virtue of liberty dwarfed piety. The antichrist became more fully identified with the dominance and exploitation of European monarchies.[24]

The French and Indian War (1754–1763) awakened prophetic writers to renew the traditional Protestant idea that the Pope is the antichrist. Some viewed the Great Awakening as revealing divine sanction for the American present and future. Political radicals revived this conviction, identifying an independent America with the New Jerusalem and the very throne of Christ.

Liberty-loving spirits imbibed zeal against tyranny from their Puritan forefathers who saw America as a new Israel.[25]

REVOLUTIONARY NATIONAL VICTORY— REVELATORY INTERNATIONAL DUTY

By the 1770s, Christian ministers had linked their millennial vision to the pursuit of American liberties. American society was to be viewed as the model for all nations aspiring to liberty. By exporting freedom values, America would be recognized as the earthly seat of Jesus' Kingdom rule.

Samuel Langdon (1723–1797), president of Harvard, spoke to the congress of the Massachusetts Bay Colony on May 13, 1775. He expressed his conviction that biblically revealed Hebraic polity represented the perfect civil republic. It was therefore worthy of emulation. A future American constitution should fully honor both the Law of Moses and the Law of Christ. This would enable future legislators to write just laws and help establish moral codes for public conduct. Israel had initially failed but still had a divine destiny. The American New Zion had likewise failed to date but could yet create a "city of righteousness" and become a "holy people." The overwhelming positive response of the Continental Congress on March 16, 1776, strengthened the earlier Puritan identification of the American Christian Zion with Israel.[26]

In 1776, Connecticut's Reverend Samuel Sherwood declared that God and all His heavenly powers were on the side of the Americans and against Great Britain—the man of sin, the antichrist. The successful establishment of American civil and religious liberties would extend to the millennial reign of Christ.[27]

When revolutionary clergy received reports of British victories, they did not despair. Instead, they spoke of the hope of Christ's soon coming. Even American losses signaled a swiftly approaching end to the tyrannical man of sin and an American victorious chorus of "Babylon the Great is fallen." Preachers like Samuel West of Boston reasoned that liberty and true religion would be banished from the earth if America lost its calling from God. America's destiny was divinely decreed. The hope for God's people centered on it.

Some three weeks after the signing of the Declaration of Independence, Timothy Dwight, grandson of Jonathan Edwards and valedictorian at Yale, declared that "that remarkable Jewish tradition" of a full millennium of "peace, purity, and felicity" would find climactic expression in America. This would commence about the year 2000. In Dwight's *The Conquest of Canaan* (1785), he indicated that just as God had carefully planned His giving of Palestine to the Jewish people, he was now bestowing North America on Americans as His final dramatic fulfillment of biblical prophecy.[28] To Dwight, America was not only the New Israel, but the base of the everlasting earthly Kingdom.

IN THE RELIGIOUS WAKE OF
THE RIGHTEOUS REVOLUTION

The United States, newly liberated from British confinements and European clerical imperialism, sensed divine ordination to inaugurate a new era of religious and civic purity. Some saw the American spread of the Gospel and republican principles leading into the millennium. Sacred faith and political liberties were practically inseparable. A new kind of eschatology was born.

American fascination with the endtimes never long subsided in succeeding generations. Americans would seek to redefine themselves and their national responsibilities to God, but the interplay of politics and the biblical hopes for the future continued to motivate Americans into the 20th century. This interplay of politics and biblical hope would mold the course of events at crucial moments in American history. Consistent themes of American eschatology included Israel's future, the antichrist and his impact, developments in the Islamic world, and timelines of prediction. Specific details and named personalities changed with each generation, but these themes remained remarkably identical.

Even American Sephardic Jewish leaders such as Gershom Seixas (1746–1816) ascribed American victory to the God of Israel. He believed that this victory was in anticipation of the ultimate liberation of the land of Israel and the soon coming of the Messiah.

Professors and preachers often linked Jewish people and Native Americans. Charles Crawford (1752–1815) advocated missions among Native Americans as a remnant of the ten lost tribes of Israel. Both sets of Israelites would return to Jerusalem around 1900 for the restoration of Israel. The American New Israel would be used of God to help effect this.

During most of the 1700s, national spiritual transformation and the restoration of the Jewish people to Zion was not heavily stressed. But the French Revolution's challenge to the papacy ignited pro-Zionist enthusiasm. Even former President John Adams wrote, "I really wish the Jews again in Judea, an independent nation."[29] Ezra Stiles, preacher and patriot, declared this would be so. Prophecies of prosperity and abundance would apply not only to millennial Israel but also to the United States. American minds would be God's instruments to evangelize the world even prior to the millennial reign of Christ.

Elhanan Winchester of New Haven envisioned the same. He believed God had smiled on America as the first nation with both civil and religious liberty. He boasted of American treatment of Jewish people, giving them the privileges of all American-born subjects. Continuing to provide them protection and liberties would assure God's blessing on America.

Right up to the Civil War, American Christians were convinced that America had a divinely established mission. American Christians would help usher in the spiritual revival of the universe. They would witness the establishment of Christ's 1,000 year reign from Zion.

19ᵀᴴ CENTURY INFLUENCES
ON PENTECOSTAL IDEOLOGY

The post-Civil War reality of evil compelled a complete reevaluation of millennial perspective and of America as the New Israel. American society's tender fabric was fiercely tested by radical changes. The new freedom of 3.5 million slaves, the complexities of Reconstruction efforts in the South, the expansive opening of the far West, political corruption, big business, inventions including the telephone and light bulb, and rapid rural migration to the cities all had a profound impact.

Postmillennialism

The Great Awakening had stimulated masses of Americans to hope with Jonathan Edwards that the millennium was about to begin.[30] Edwards' postmillennialism was quite different from later Pentecostal millennialism. He did not expect any restoration of spiritual gifts. He anticipated a gradual increase of the graces of God's presence. Christ would come only to a universe eager to welcome Him. Meanwhile, change would be gradual as Christians could govern through existing institutions. Postmillennialism was optimistic, socially comfortable, and spiritually forward moving.

By the time of the Second Great Awakening (1800–1805), progressive millennialism was standardized in the Protestant South. Southern Presbyterians believed the soul-saving institution of the Church was preparing mankind for the Second Coming. Godliness and morality would universally intensify under Christian missions. Governments and social institutions would experience Christian reform. Wars, vices, and other social evils would be liquidated. Universal prosperity would follow. Life expectancy would soon exceed the century mark.[31]

Formal churches of the 1840s North rejoiced in the social progress in America as the nation benefitted from the efforts of volunteer benevolent and reform societies. Southern formal churches believed the world would steadily improve until the Second Coming. Many Presbyterians welcomed a calm, steady, and hopefully uneventful thousand-year universal betterment. The world seemed to be constantly improving with daily material progress, self-betterment, and personal freedom. Yet opposing viewpoints held by premillennialists flew in the face of the social confidence of the more formal churches. New England Baptist Abraham Cummings warned in 1799 that Christ would suddenly appear for world judgment. In the 1830s, Methodist John Hersey proclaimed the millennium would commence with Christ's soon coming reign in Zion. In spite of postmillennial optimists, premillennial prophecies of doom became more pervasive and persuasive.[32]

The Wesleyan Contribution

Methodism's perfectionism was a natural partner to Edwardian postmillennialism. Together they fueled the optimism of the new American nation. Methodists were involved in evangelism and committed to the full restoration of pristine New Testament faith. However, historical events failed to support postmillennial dreams. Eschatology needed the revitalization found by recognizing that the Second Coming is to be premillennial and will, in fact, bring in the millennium. It would be sovereignly timed and would need nothing from humankind. It could occur at any moment. Thus, premillennialism found new and eager support among many previously disheartened Christians.[33] Methodist William Arthur published the popular *Tongue of Fire* in 1856 which anticipated a grand revival and the restoration of early Pentecostal experience with tongues of fire.

The Oberlin Perfectionists

Charles Finney in his Oberlin Evangelist wrote that widespread holiness would precede the millennium. In the same periodical, Henry Cowles suggested in 1841 that radical changes in his day portended a new prophetic era. The Holy Spirit would be given so that widespread holiness would become the Christian norm. The Jewish people would become spiritually redeemed in Christ and national Israel would be restored.[34]

Cowles believed that by its spiritual neglect the Church could delay the millennium. It must fully cooperate with the Holy Spirit and be fully anticipating the arriving millennium. His sermons on sanctification spoke of the baptism of the Holy Spirit. He used what would become standard Pentecostal vocabulary to speak of the general revival that saw its archetype in the Day of Pentecost.[35]

The writings of John Morgan, a contributor to the first volume of the 1845 *Oberlin Quarterly Review,* were also crucial to the Pentecostal question. He taught that the Pentecostal experience of the early Church would be re-experienced by all the sanctified. He distinguished this from the wooing experience of the Spirit so vital to personal salvation.[36] Finney believed the Spirit's fullness should be normative for Christians. The Oberlin team used the terms baptism and filling with the Holy Spirit for the second experience they espoused.[37]

SOCIAL CHANGE
IN THE LATTER HALF OF 19TH CENTURY

From the Civil War to 1900, social, political, and economic norms were being changed. Philosophical and religious thought seemed to be shaking the ground beneath the American worldview. Industrialization and urbanization were impacting social patterns. The wealthy assumed little responsibility for the welfare of the poor. Immigrants were pouring into the nation, providing cheap labor. The working poor were restless, living in crowded cities. Within a few years, Southern Presbyterians became premillennialists believing that humankind was sinking into an evil abyss that only the Second Coming could remedy.[38]

Postmillennialism faced multiple challenges. American religion was experiencing the influx of Roman Catholics and Lutherans as well as the immigration of European Jewish people and other non-Christians. Biblical criticism was on the rise, and Darwinism was challenging the biblical creation account and the general reliability of Scripture. Christian victims of such social upheaval viewed their world as in steady decline.

Yet revivalism grew rapidly among the unchurched and followed the rural migration to the cities. As if the prelude to Pentecostalism, shouting and rhythmic singing accompanied the main event—preaching.[39] In the absence of folk socialization that rural living afforded, city revival services became a common form of social recreation. Church brothers and sisters were glad alternates for natural family left on the farm.

JOHN N. DARBY AND CYRUS I. SCOFIELD— PROPHETS OF PREMILLENNIAL DISPENSATIONALISM

John Nelson Darby (1800–1882) began his ministry as an Anglican in Ireland. Mid-career he developed a bleak assessment of the established Church. Embracing austerity, simplicity in worship, discipline, and the imminent Second Coming, he helped found the Plymouth Brethren. He despaired of the New Testament Church restorationism that would prove vital to the later Pentecostal revival. But his premillennialism included a secret rapture of Christians, the Battle of Armageddon, the Second Coming, and the Jewish regathering to Zion.[40]

Cyrus Ingerson Scofield (1843–1921), an American lawyer, attempted to simplify the prophetic teachings of the Bible. His dispensationalism saw no link between God's people in the Old and New Testaments. The Hebrew Bible applied only to Israel. Prophecies of a coming millennial kingdom applied only to Israel, not to the Church. Even the Sermon on the Mount had at best a moral application for Christians. Its chief application would be to Jewish people in the Jewish millennial kingdom.

Darby's dispensationalism was soon promoted by many Evangelicals. It was catapulted to greater acceptance by the publication of *Scofield's Reference Bible* in 1909. Their dispensationalism taught that the current "Church Age" would soon end in failure. Only then would the King of Israel reoffer and finally establish the promised kingdom for Israel. This would bring fulfillment to the biblical plan for the ages and the nations would reach their eternal destinies. Over time, more Americans relinquished the myth of unique Anglo significance and anticipated a speedy conclusion to human and salvation history.

According to the dispensationalist scheme, the Church Age will end in dismal failure. It had only been a parenthesis in God's eternal plan for Israel. The soon coming of Christ called for evangelism to spare all nations God's eternal wrath. Some dispensationalists held that Americans needed both sanctification and boldness from the Holy Spirit for evangelism. But only after the rapture of authentic Christians to Heaven would God be free to restore His severed relations with Israel. After a seven-year period of chastening, nationally restored Israel would welcome the Messiah Jesus. He would then commence His thousand-year reign over humankind in fulfillment of God's covenants and promises.

Scofield held that Acts 11:14 rather than Acts 2 marked the pivotal change in God's economy. Until this point, the Gospel was offered only to Jewish people. The Holy Spirit was first given here to non-Jews by apostolic mediation. From this point forward, however, the Holy Spirit was given without delay to non-Jews in response to simple faith in Christ. The dispensation of Law had ended in favor of the dispensation of grace. Therefore, everything in the four Gospels and in the Book of Acts up to 11:44 had been issued or done under the dispensation of Law.[41] Israel's salvation could only occur when Israel had a second opportunity to embrace Jesus' then renewed Kingdom offer subsequent to the Church Age.

ESSENTIAL DISPENSATIONALISM AND ISRAEL

Dispensationalism, with its bleak assessment concerning the coming failure of the Church Age, and Pentecostalism, with its inherent upbeat enthusiasm for Church restoration to its Book of Acts victorious origins, are incompatible at their cores. Yet dispensationalism did have an immense impact on Pentecostalism. Not until the latter third of the 20th century did many recognize the opposing nature of these two systems. Until then, many Pentecostals freely used the Scofield Reference Bible and taught Bible college courses advocating dispensationalism "with [a Pentecostalist] edge." Along with this, they emphasized the soon coming of Christ to the restored Jewish State in Zion.

Postmillennialism's eschatological "Achilles heel" was that it raised hopes that simply did not materialize. How might millennial hope remain alive? Dispensationalists answered by rescheduling the Second Coming for the commencement of the millennium. Jesus would inaugurate the thousand year reign without waiting for sympathetic supporters to ready His throne. The onus was thus lifted off disappointed postmillennialists and placed on God. What man could not do, God would do at the moment of His own choosing and divine pleasure.

Historical Premillennialism

Historical premillennialists taught that the cross brought Jewish people and Gentiles together as both were equally needing God's grace. Israel's millennial kingdom experience would not exclude the Church.[42] In fact, according to this view, the death and resurrection of Christ had transferred the spiritual covenant with God to the Church. Israel could be restored only when she accepted the work of the cross.[43]

Israel and the Church

John Darby's breaks with historical premillennialism were few, but his greatest rupture was the radical divorce between the functions of Israel and the Church. They were to be forever separate. The Church could not impinge upon Israel or benefit at the expense of Israel's relationship to God. There was no biblical "spiritual Israel." The promises of God should not be spiritualized or allegorized out of meaningful existence. The promises to Israel remained inviolate.[44] As previous dispensations ended in ruin, the Church Age would likewise end with minimal impact on a world full of rebels.

For Darby, the spiritually restored Jewish people and nation-state, rather than the Church, would bring universal blessings on humankind. The Abrahamic covenant (see Gen. 17:6-8) assured that Abraham's seed would be a great nation inheriting Canaan for eternity. The Jewish role in the redemption of humankind in the millennium would be the literal fulfillment of both Abrahamic and Davidic covenants. They would not be Church-related.

This radical distinction between Israel and the Church compelled Darby to invent the idea that the Church Age was a parenthesis in God's program while the kingdom was postponed because Jewish leadership had rejected Christ. God's program's outward structure was suspended while Gentiles filled the time gap. But God would fulfill His promises, and in the uniquely Jewish kingdom, Israel would radiate universal glory. Thus, because of Darby, premillennialists began looking to Israel, not America, as the catalyst to the fulfillment of Bible prophecy. So the ideal of America as the "New Israel" dramatically declined.[45]

Despair of the Church and Society

To Darby, the Church was hopelessly corrupted by the dictates of human government.[46] It was further degenerating all the time. It was not the work of the Church to effect moral reform.[47] Any Christian attempt to restore the ruined Church to its New Testament form was doomed to failure. God had never restored previous dispensations to their original condition. God would provide a new beginning, a new dispensation to perpetuate His program of salvation history. The next grand dispensation was, to Darby, the Messianic kingdom dispensation. Darby did not accept any Church responsibility for improving the state of the world. Nevertheless, he did provide incentive for evangelism to ready humankind for the Second Coming and judgment. The eternal state of lost souls was the burning issue.

C. Norman Kraus pointed out that dispensationalism embraced a pagan Greek philosophy of history with each historical cycle ending in apostasy and judgment. This fairly limited God's intervention in history to His launching of yet another dispensational cycle.[48] This is in stark contrast to the later Pentecostal perspective of a highly active God working in the world of space and time, in and through His people.

OTHER AMERICAN VOICES

As ordinary Americans were sensing the imminent collapse of the world, some home-grown American "prophets" seized the opportunity to provide spiritual direction. Joseph Smith (1805–1844), the founder of Mormonism, claimed to receive in 1831 an angelic revelation indicating in part that the Jewish people should flee to Jerusalem. In 1843, he stated the return of the Jewish people and the restoration of the land would predate the Second Coming. Charles Taze Russell (1852–1915), the founder of the Jehovah's Witnesses, saw Zionism as a fulfillment of biblical prophecy. He circulated his ideas broadly through the Watch Tower Bible and Tract Society of New York.

The imprint of the Jewish people and the Hebrew Bible on the American religious public was profound. A Jewish return to Zion often was center stage among home-grown cults and sects firmly established in America. It was a focal point for theological discussion and long-term planning. It is no wonder that Evangelicalism and American Pentecostalism would continue to place importance on the reconstruction of the Jewish State. But American Pentecostals would have their own unique enthusiasm for the Zionist cause.

William Blackstone's *Jesus Is Coming*, published in 1878, supported Darby's dispensationalism. It was widely distributed in the 1890s. In 1908, a wealthy sympathizer reissued 700,000 copies in thirty-one languages for the benefit of religious leaders. *Jesus Is Coming* generated much Evangelical enthusiasm for the reestablishment of a Jewish State in Zion.[49] Blackstone's work presented legal and historical arguments in support of Zionism and called for Christian compassion for Jewish suffering.

In 1891, Blackstone presented to U.S. President Benjamin Harrison 413 Christian and Jewish signatures calling for an international conference on the currently bleak Jewish situation. Since Jewish people were already indicating a desire to be a nation again, he spoke of the incipient Zionist objective to return Jewish people to the land of their fathers. He realized Jewish discussions regarding a return to Zion had been primarily of a secular character but believed restoration to the land would ultimately bring spiritual restoration and the Jewish people would once again walk with God.[50]

PREMILLENNIALISM AND THE ENDTIMES

Premillennialism existed before the dramatic rise of dispensationalism, but it was the aggressive teaching of dispensationalism through Bible and prophecy conferences that provided it with greater visibility.[51] In 1878, Christians suspicious of the truth of postmillennialism began sponsoring premillennial prophecy conferences. They believed the world would never experience redemption based on scientific progress or committed mission enterprise. The first International Prophecy Conference was held in New York City on October 30, 1878.

Resolutions passed at the end of the conference affirmed the absolute authority and literal fulfillment of the whole Bible, Christ's soon coming, the ongoing evil decline of society, and the Church's need both to pray and work. A second prophecy conference in Niagara in 1885 sought to reinforce the view of progressive evil to the end of the Church Age.[52] Recent years of theological liberalism in seminaries and pulpits conditioned the participants to hostility toward a "hell-bent" society. They saw evangelism, not as a means of revitalizing society, but rather as the means to reach a "select few."[53]

Premillennialism offered great appeal on the basis of current events, "the signs of the times." These included secular and religious reports of Jewish people returning to Palestine. Multiple examples of Jewish people coming to Christ suggested a foretaste of the millennial Jewish harvest. The increase in foreign missions was important since Jesus proclaimed the end would come when the Gospel had been proclaimed to all nations.[54]

In 1901, Cyrus Scofield and Arno Gaebelein (1861–1945) formed a new conference organization, the Sea Cliff Bible Conference which lasted ten years. This group then planned a grander prophecy conference for Chicago in 1914 and New York. Their work was so effective that dispensationalism became virtually identified with premillennialism.

Evangelical revivalism shifted from postmillennialism to premillennialism between the time of Charles Finney (1792–1875) and Dwight Moody (1837–1899). This is one of the most staggering developments in 19th-century America. Instead of the Church enjoying the kingdom with Christ, dispensationalism gave the kingdom to the Jewish people alone. The Church had a very different spiritual character and destiny.[55]

Restorationism

Restorationists expressed their hopes in historical terms—the "apostolic morning" that had been lost during the "papal night" but followed by the "reformation's cloudy afternoon." The late 1800s would soon see the restoration of New Testament faith. In an era where the social importance of the individual was otherwise decreasing, Evangelicals were preparing to take heroic stands in advance of the Second Coming. Involvement in kingdom enterprise provided spiritual status and personal value.[56]

Jewish Restoration as Catalyst to Expectation of Fulfilled Prophecy

Evangelicals who believed Jesus would soon come watched the pre-Zionist stirrings in the Holy Land. They also anticipated the spiritual transformation of the Jewish people at the Second Coming. Missionaries to the Jewish people helped American Christians focus on Zion as the site of the fulfillment of prophecy. Protestant literalists saw no reason to doubt the full restoration of Zion in space and time.[57]

Pentecostal Restoration as Catalyst to Expectation of Fulfilled Prophecy

Edward Irving (1792–1834), a Presbyterian minister in London, gathered a following through his charismatic preaching. He expected Jesus to come soon. In his 1828 lectureship in Edinburgh on the Book of Revelation, he offered the view that speaking in tongues (glossolalia) was a key sign of the soon coming of Christ foretold by Jesus Himself.

The mounting restorationist theme in the 1880s and 1890s included faith healing. Physical healings as well as spiritual healings were declared to be part of the accomplished work of the cross. Some disputed popular preacher-teacher A.B. Simpson, saying his view that gifts of healing were available would suggest to some that the dispensationally obsolete use of speaking in tongues is still relevant as well. Simpson responded by insisting that tongues would indeed be restored to a repentant Church for use in the spread of the Gospel.[58]

Dispensationalist "Baptism in the Holy Spirit"

Dwight L. Moody, Reuben A. Torrey, A.J. Gordon, A.T. Pierson, and A.B. Simpson, all popular non-Wesleyan preachers, strongly promoted dispensationalism. They also held that the Holy Spirit was given first to purify and secondly to empower the believer for global evangelism. Successful witness would require the baptism in the Holy Spirit to give power for service. They strongly encouraged any believer not baptized in the Holy Spirit to stop everything until "clothed with power from on high." This would be a personal crisis spiritual experience.[59]

Moody, in 1881, commenced annual summer conferences at Northfield, Massachusetts. Their purpose was to explore the relationship between the believer and the Holy Spirit. Over the following two decades, thousands claimed to be filled or baptized in the Holy Spirit. By 1886, the Northfield conferences added a foreign missions emphasis and popularized a host of new gospel songs centering on the end-time outpourings of the Holy Spirit. Moody and Torrey believed every believer should be Spirit-baptized to win souls to Christ.[60]

What Evidence of the Spirit's Baptism?

Neither Torrey nor his contemporaries ventured to advocate any single evidence for the baptism in the Holy Spirit.[61] John Darby had taught that the present age would transition into a new era of the Holy Spirit. The Keswick camp from England picked up on this Holy Spirit emphasis to advocate that the rising desire for holiness was evidence of Christ's soon coming.[62] The "sanctified" should seek to demonstrate their separation from worldly society by abstaining from pork, coffee, alcohol, and tobacco. Attending theater, dancing, mixed swimming, wearing neckties, spectator sports, and women's hair cutting were all forbidden.[63]

Early Puritans and Methodists were serious about having spiritual assurance. The enthusiasm of the revivalists was often related to their inner sense of "blessed assurance." Early Methodists agreed that reformation of the Church would only last if God would pour out His Spirit on His people. Christians should spare no effort to preach and pray down the Spirit's outpouring.[64]

In the late 1800s, the matter of "evidence" of spiritual blessing was taken even more seriously. Hannah Whitall Smith quoted a testimony of one who said the baptism in the Holy Spirit was a physical thing, felt by delightful thrills going through the Christian from head to toe. At the same time, Holiness leadership began warning against any physical or emotional signs of spiritual blessing. By 1891, Methodist Asbury Lowery published a strong protest against any outward signs altogether.[65]

Apostolic "Baptism in the Holy Spirit"

Reuben A. Torrey's *Baptism With the Holy Spirit* (1897) addressed key issues related to spiritual experience and its evidence. Plainly the apostles knew when their commanded waiting in Jerusalem should end. What had been their sign? He went on to insist Spirit baptism was clearly distinct from regeneration. This spiritual baptism occupied the recipient with spiritual pursuits and was absolutely mandatory for every kind of Christian ministry.[66] Moody also taught a distinct gift of the Holy Spirit is vital for anointed and qualified Christian service.[67] By 1900 a significant minority of American Evangelicals believed a distinct experience with the Holy Spirit was essential to the fulfilling of the Great Commission before Jesus would come.

Yet American Evangelicals could not be oblivious to the domestic and international events around them. At the turn of the 20th century, the dream of successful missionary enterprise showed signs of potential realization. University students chanted of the successful evangelization of the world in their own generation. But new materialistic meanings were also read into the mission of America.

CONCLUSION

American Pentecostalist ideas would be formed at the beginning of the 20th century as the result of several historical streams. These ideas would include the everlasting hope for a nationally restored Jewish people in Zion.

Chapter 2

FRATERNAL TWIN INFANTS:

Pentecostalism and Zionism (1901–1917)

To discover the vital link between Zionism and the Pentecostal movement takes careful scrutiny of the motifs behind the theological formation of this relationship. Pentecostalism was formed in the caldron of religious controversy and social upheaval. Their highly charged spiritual experiences located biblical and extra-biblical evidence of their end-time legitimacy in their fellow modern traveler, Zionism.

Early Pentecostals saw the "end time" as God's moment in time for the restoration of both Israel and the Church. The brightly relit torch of New Testament Christianity would shine across a darkened world in momentary expectation of the Second Coming. The flash of this expectation accompanied the flare of Pentecostal experience.

Most of the Pentecostal belief system was not new. Many Evangelicals were already strongly promoting salvation, healing, baptism in the Holy Spirit, Christ's return, and Israel's ultimate restoration. Speaking in tongues as the initial evidence of Spirit baptism was the Pentecostal distinctive teaching. This glossolalia teaching generated division between Pentecostals and the rest of Evangelical Christianity, yet it enjoyed widespread appeal in the midst of American social changes.[1]

Though birthed among many dispensationalist camps, Pentecostals emphasized present "end-time" restoration of apostolic Christianity before Christ's soon return. When Evangelicals and Holiness groups reacted negatively, Pentecostals felt the need to respond speedily to legitimize their position.

> "Latter Rain" writings, like David Myland's in 1910, took a stand against the Holiness movement's identification of the baptism in the Holy Spirit with "entire sanctification" or "Christian perfection." Pentecostals perceived the restoration of spiritual gifts including speaking in tongues showed that God was indeed restoring the Church to its apostolic origins. The Church needed this special Spirit-anointing for global evangelism before God's wrath would be poured out in judgment on the nations.[2]

PENTECOSTAL APPEAL TO LOWER CLASSES: "THE VISION OF THE DISINHERITED"

The years 1890–1925 brought profound economic and social changes to America. The depression of 1893–1896 caused class conflict. The succeeding years saw new developments in urbanization, massive immigration, the Spanish-American war, and an increase in an anti-supernatural social gospel.[3]

Early Pentecostals came from broad racial, regional, and educational backgrounds. Most, however, were poor. Many were uprooted from the quiet peace of farm life and forced into overcrowded city dwellings. Rural societies were also disillusioned socially. Modernist unbelief brought spiritual loss to many. Those who still believed in a supernatural God were drawn to the Pentecostals.[4]

People who felt hostile to a society inflicting injustices on them saw in Pentecostalism a new source of energy. They could use the revolutionizing power of the baptism in the Holy Spirit to function as God's holy instruments of prophetic judgment on the world.

Mainstream historical denominations were ignoring revivalism as simply old-fashioned. But by 1905 Methodists' official journals wrote that a powerful revival was seeping into every corner of America. Presbyterians also observed that masses of Americans were anticipating a wonderful outpouring of the Holy Spirit. A "new spiritual epoch" was reported in Kansas City.[5]

In 1905, Baptists published accounts of new spiritual life in churches and Bible colleges. In Dixon, Illinois, all the major denominations cooperated in a "cyclonic revival" under the ministry of Billy Sunday, baseball star turned evangelist. Southern Baptists of Paducah, Kentucky, described their own "great Pentecostal revival," lasting from November 1905 through March 1906.[6]

Revivals impacted both Whites and African Americans. In Ohio, revivals touched 50 congregations in Dayton alone. Methodists in Michigan reported outpourings that awakened entire towns. Churches in Saginaw, Owosso, and Tuscola were filled with "Pentecostal power" for five weeks.[7]

The climate for revivalism was red hot. News of revivals in Topeka in 1901 and Los Angeles in 1906 drew many of the socially disadvantaged to Pentecostalism with high-spirited eagerness. These included drunkards, gamblers, loose women, and unbelievers.[8] Without the need for church hierarchy or priestly class, people of many colors celebrated a common brotherhood. Instead of religious programming, they simply "let the Spirit move them." To marginalized people, Pentecostalism provided a grand sense of belonging to a new, far more meaningful society. There was no color line, and many Pentecostals conducted multiple services in various languages.

Pentecostals viewed their movement as the divine restoration of the full Gospel. This helped give them a sense of identity and purpose as well as personal peace and the confidence of ultimate victory.[9] They felt speaking in tongues, exorcisms, and healings were more important than trying to influence politics or the economy. Only God could improve a world in rebellion to Him. Christ's coming and the millennium would be God's instruments to initiate a just society.

Readiness of Pentecostals to move from group to group or from dogma to dogma reflected their seekers' mode of life.[10] Widespread proliferation of Pentecostal fellowships in public halls and small storefronts testified to their eagerness for personal involvement and their quest for ever-grander faith experiences.

Within one year of the 1906 Azusa Street revival, Pentecostalism claimed ten to fifteen thousand adherents. This increased tenfold by 1916. Its greatest growth would come between 1910 and 1950. With few exceptions, such as college and Bible-school trained Elmer Fisher and seminary trained J. Narver Gortner, Pentecostal leadership came largely from young men, who like most Americans, came from rural surroundings. Thus, most did not have much social status.[11]

EARLY PENTECOSTAL VOICES

Pentecostalism arose at the turn of the 20th century as a consummation of earlier teachings by restorationists and Holiness preachers. They regretted the Church's departure from the simplicity and purity of New Testament Christianity. They yearned for a return to the standards of the Book of Acts.

Charles Parham

Charles Fox Parham (1873–1929), a Midwest Methodist evangelist, founded Bethel Bible College in Topeka, Kansas. He taught that speaking in tongues is the initial evidence of the baptism in the Holy Spirit. The gift of tongues immediately became the chief distinguishing characteristic of Pentecostal teaching. This brought a fair amount of derision and contempt from the rest of American Christianity.

For Parham, no theology was needed, just the enlightenment of the Spirit in reading the Bible. The same Spirit who inspired Holy Writ could also inspire its proper interpretation. Unlike the "dead" churches, the operation of the gifts of the Spirit in Pentecostalism demonstrated the Spirit's endorsement of the Pentecostal message.

Parham believed the chief purpose of tongues speaking was the successful evangelization of the globe in all languages, the ultimate sign of the Second Coming. He based his belief on Acts 2:6-8. He thought it was a waste of missionary time and resources to learn new languages.[12] He failed to see that discipleship involved teaching, answering questions, and establishing churches. Parham's insistence on tongues as the initial evidence of the baptism in the Holy Spirit, however, became the official position of the Assembles of God after 1914.

In keeping with his end-time restoration of apostolic faith, Parham lectured publicly in support of Theodor Herzl's Zionist hope for a Jewish State. He was able to reconcile this with his idea that Anglo-Saxons were destined to dominate the globe. He saw migration from India to Britain of "Isaac's Sons (read "Saxons") as ultimately leading to the English Puritan migration to the New World. His lectures on Zionism were popular, and he would frequently preach wearing symbolic Palestinian clothing.

Parham, in his biweekly publication, Apostolic Faith, taught that Spirit baptism "sealed the bride" for the marriage supper of the Lamb. It also provided the only escape from the "Great Tribulation." Spirit baptism with tongues speaking would also seal 144,000 Jewish witnesses who would be active during the tribulation period.[13]

Parham took the Pentecostal message to Alexander Dowie in Zion, Illinois, in the fall of 1906. The Pentecostal constituency he created there would later yield a crop of leaders for the newly formed Assemblies of God in 1914. Parham had a history of physical and mental breakdowns that eventually limited his audience.[14] His protégé, William Seymour, would soon eclipse his ministry, much to everyone's surprise and to Parham's discontent.

William Seymour

William Seymour (1870–1922), African American pastor at the Azusa Street Mission in Los Angeles, spent from November 1905 to February 1906 at Parham's Houston Bible school. Seymour's opening days of the Azusa Street revival in April 1906 coincided with the devastating San Francisco earthquake. Religious interest quaked as well in response to the Los Angeles Daily Times coverage of the revival. Those participating included people of many races, including Jewish people.[15] They were convinced God's Shechinah glory was in their meetings. Miracles persuaded them that the power of the 1st-century Church was being restored and Jesus would soon return.

Many of the new participants said their baptism in the Spirit with speaking in tongues transcended any previous spiritual experience they had known.[16] This claim would meet with religious hostility.

The mixed racial participation, the speaking in tongues, and shouting and rolling on the floor evoked both curiosity and mockery. But new arrivals kept coming with great expectation. Probably as many as 13,000 people were baptized in the Holy Spirit in the first year of the revival.[17] These included a number of Holiness leaders. But the insistence on tongues as the initial evidence of the baptism in the Holy Spirit brought a major breach between Pentecostals and most Holiness groups.

Pentecostals believed the Holy Spirit would soon speak in all the languages of the world through God's children. Even as the 1st-century Jewish Pentecostals had spread the Gospel, so too would the latter-day Pentecostals. They eagerly participated in world missions to expedite Christ's return. Simultaneously they expressed enthusiasm for the Zionist cause as a "sign of the times." The movement coming out of Azusa Street quickly became one of the fastest growing movements in the world, with outbreaks in Chicago, Toronto, Europe, and India. It reaped both respect and fear from other religious groups.

EARLY PENTECOSTAL RESTORATIONISM, GLOSSOLALIA, AND ZIONISM

Riding high on the national narrative of a "Christian America," Pentecostals viewed themselves as the marines leading the Christian light and freedom brigade in a world full of spiritual darkness and bondage. While most of the historical churches ignored them, leading Evangelicals violently opposed them. Pentecostals responded by simply withdrawing their memberships from Evangelical and Holiness churches and forming a wide variety of Pentecostal congregations.[18]

Evangelical as well as liberal Christian groups generally had no experience with or exposure to contemporary Pentecostals. Yet they dubbed supposedly extreme Pentecostal emotionalism as mad or pathological. Pentecostal welcoming of women preachers also caused ridicule. As early as 1907, Arthur Pierson, a highly influential Evangelical cautioned against what he called Pentecostal excesses. Reuben A. Torrey totally rejected tongues as the initial evidence of the baptism in the Holy Spirit. Harry Ironside, another popular Bible teacher, also condemned Pentecostalism as unwholesome.[19]

Pentecostal focus on tongues speaking as an Acts 2 "upper room" experience also alarmed millennial dispensationalists on another count. The dispensationalists expected the Church Age to end in failure rather than in Church renewal to a Book of Acts form. But Pentecostals continued to fan the flames of spiritual revival in direct relation to their premillennialism. They viewed speaking in tongues and divine healing as signs of the last days. Jesus would come soon. Dispensationalists also contended that miracles had ceased with the apostles, and therefore the Pentecostal movement was not authentic. By 1912, A.B. Simpson labeled the tongues-as-the-evidence-of-Spirit-baptism teaching as divisive and evil producing. On April 13, 1914, Simpson's Christian and Missionary Alliance officially repudiated tongues as the initial evidence of Spirit baptism. Meanwhile, the historic churches came to brand Pentecostalism as of the devil.

Disappointed that the Second Coming was delayed and keenly feeling the rejection of their closest religious peers, Pentecostal inner-group solidarity grew in importance. They taught that resistance to the Pentecostal emphasis was resistance to God Himself. But better apologetics were desperately needed.

The Essence of Pentecostal Restorationism

The essence of Pentecostal restorationism needs to be explained before seeking to understand its relationship to the Jewish people. Instead of the earlier Evangelical hope for gradual transformation of the world, or the dispensationalist expectation of ultimate Church Age failure, the Pentecostals believed the Second Coming would immediately remedy the God-defiant condition of the world and transform it into a Garden of Eden.

During this time Pentecostals believed they owed nothing to the spiritually darkened past of church history or to the colossal errors so characteristic of historical theology. It was the Book of Acts alone that provided the blueprint for modern apostolic Christianity. In these Last Days, the Church was now being reestablished in New Testament purity and renewed to its God-intended spiritual power.

Expectation of Christ's soon return compelled Pentecostals to action. God's wrath would shortly be poured out on the nations, but all should be given fair opportunity to repent and believe. Like the Hebrew prophets before them, an urgent sense of prophetic duty rested on these "last days" Pentecostals. They had received Spirit baptism with signs, wonders, and miracles confirming the Gospel they preached. But a second key and corresponding confirmation of the Pentecostal Gospel and the Second Coming was the return of the Jewish people to Zion.[20]

In Defense of Glossolalia: The Latter Rain

Speaking in tongues needed a strong defense against Christian hostility if Pentecostalism was to survive. Church history shows it was extensively used until the 3rd century when tongues-speaking Gnostics and Montanists were marked as heretical. But in the 1600s, tongues speaking reappeared among Quakers and French Huguenots. But the gift did not come to stay until 1900.[21]

When the use of the gift of tongues as a preaching vehicle for spreading the Gospel did not materialize, Pentecostals began searching for other explanations and meanings. Without its distinctive, Pentecostalism would fall off the religious horizon. But their pragmatic urge pushed them to do whatever was necessary to accomplish their movement's purposes.[22] They felt at liberty to use Pentecostal ideas in Pentecostal ways.[23]

Criticism and persecution energized them to defend and crystallize their beliefs. They defended themselves as a heroic minority stemming the tide of Christian resistance. Martin Luther, John Wesley, and others had likewise been condemned by many Christians of their own eras. But Pentecostals became increasingly intolerant. They openly expressed hostilities toward Roman Catholics and "cold, dead" churches. They saw religious form and ceremony as enemies to the genuine worship of God. Ecumenical attempts at promoting unity among all the churches were dubbed religious Babylonianism.

At the same time, they presented an optimistic and aggressive vision of revitalization that would ready humankind for the return of Jesus. All people could still find personal renewal in God and spiritual empowerment, but all beliefs and practices needed to be brought into conformity to the standards of the Book of Acts. They boldly blurred the distinction between laity and clergy. Anyone spiritually prompted could enter and lead worship without regard for religious edifice or decorum.[24] Many who witnessed the erosion of American cultural values found life's meaning in Pentecostal restorationism. It gave them a new sense of identity, purpose, and self-worth.

Pentecostal Restorationism's Link With Zionism: The Latter Rain

Pentecostals espoused that the "Former Rain" issued with the descent of the Holy Spirit on the Day of Pentecost in Acts 2 was now followed by its counterpart experience, the outpouring of the "Latter Rain" in these last days of time. What was needed was evidence that the Pentecostal perception was accurate.

One striking world event in the first decade of the 20th century helped make the Pentecostal revival distinct from previous spiritual renewals. Jewish people were now returning to Zion in significant numbers. Against this backdrop, Pentecostals envisioned a speedy restoration of all things to both the Church and national Israel. Just as Zion was in the process of reconstruction, apostolic spiritual gifts were now present after long centuries of disuse to refortify Christ's New Testament church. Pentecostals believed God could not break His word to the Hebrew patriarchs and prophets. He would indeed regather His Chosen Jewish People to the Messiah Jesus seated on His international throne in Jerusalem. Both Zionism and Pentecostal "latter rain" experiences pointed to this pending eschatological reality.

Several key people contributed to Latter Rain theology in relation to Zionism. F.A. Bright in 1904 wrote that the Jewish people were still beloved of God. The land would be redeemed by large-scale Zionist colonizing efforts. Many wealthy Americans Jews were already returning to Zion. Jewish people and "real Christians" were providing money so others could return. Carefully chosen craftsmen would soon begin national reconstruction of a model society. Even though Zionists did not speak of the Messiah, the prophecy of Ezekiel's dry bones was coming to pass. Israel would finally look to God.[25]

In the same year William T. MacArthur wrote of his personal admiration of Theodor Herzl, the so-called father of modern Zionism, he noted that in most of Europe, civil liberties enabled Jewish populations, education, and influence to grow. He wrote also that God would judge all nations that abused Israel. Because rainfall charting showed intensified rainfall in Palestine, MacArthur thought this corresponded to intensive outpourings of the Spirit in His restoration ministry. Also, by adding the 1260 years of Daniel 12:7 to a.d. 637, the year Muslims captured Jerusalem, MacArthur found the total, 1897, was the year modern Zionism had arisen. Zionism, he insisted, was God's instrument to regather Israel. Then Gentiles would lose preeminence as Zion would be restored. Jesus would return and launch the millennium, His thousand year reign out of Zion.[26]

George F. Taylor (1881–1934), an early leader of the Pentecostal Holiness Church, wrote a ringing defense of the Pentecostal experience in 1907. His stand for tongues as the initial evidence proved highly useful for all Pentecostals. He said the cycle of apostolic restoration had been in motion for centuries. Martin Luther, John Wesley, and the teachings of divine healing and premillennialism all met with ecclesiastical attack, and contempt for Pentecost would be no different.[27]

Bennett F. Lawrence, who later became one of the founders of the Assemblies of God, wrote in 1909 that, at the same time as the Pentecostal revival, Jewish people were returning to their land. Literal latter rain was falling on Palestine even as the spiritual latter rain was falling on Pentecostals.[28]

David W. Myland (1858–1943) composed the first widely distributed Pentecostal theology, *The Latter Rain Covenant and Pentecostal Power.* An ordained Methodist, he supported the continued use of spiritual gifts. In 1912 he founded the Gibeah Bible School in Plainfield, Indiana. J. Roswell Flower and Alice Reynolds Flower were ordained there in 1913. Myland became a regular contributor to the Flower-edited *Christian Evangel* and later to the *Pentecostal Evangel*, the official organ of the Assemblies of God.

Pentecostals quickly elevated Myland's teachings to the level of Luther's and Wesley's. They considered the Pentecostal outpouring epoch-making in the annals of God's eternal program. Jerusalem would be the future headquarters of the Jewish people. The city would be divided as in David's day: the general city, the temple mount, and the Messiah King's residence on Mount Zion. Myland was certain of the direct prophetic correspondence between what God was doing with national Israel and what He was doing with the Church.[29]

William H. Cossum (b. 1863) accepted John Nelson Darby's dispensational idea that the divine program for the Jewish people had been interrupted by rejecting the kingdom and would be resumed only at Christ's return. All Israel would then experience unity around their Messiah. A Pentecostal outpouring would then revitalize Israel. Cossum, however, stressed the significance of the study of prophecy. The modern return to Zion was numerically greater than the ancient return from Babylon. God had only delayed His program for Israel. He had not forfeited it. All Israel would ultimately become Pentecostal. The Zionist movement was destined to succeed. But it would take fiery trials to purify the Jewish people, bring them to repentance, and reach their prophetic goal.[30]

In his *The Second Coming of Jesus* (1916), George F. Taylor contended that the promises of God for the perpetuity of Jerusalem were meaningful, not mere word pictures. He saw an eternal link between Jesus, Zion, and the Jewish people. He took the Book of Revelation literally rather than allegorically as the liberals did. Israel would be restored, but not necessarily before the Second Coming.

In summary, the Latter Rain message of the Fall's rainfall bringing the culminating harvest as opposed to the Spring rains when the plowing season only begins was a favorite Pentecostal apologetic. Acts 2 represented the Spring's initiating rainfall for the agricultural year, but the 20t- century Pentecostals were the current beneficiaries of the harvest-bound "Latter Rain." This restorationist theme was undergirded by the assurance of the Second Coming and by speaking in tongues. The returning Messiah would rule the universe from the Davidic throne in Jerusalem. Since time was so short, Gospel ambassadors must be spiritually equipped to do a "quick work."

The Balfour Declaration of 1917 ignited premillennial expectations as nothing else had. Suddenly the reestablishment of a Jewish national homeland was more than a dream. The Jewish State would soon be a reality with all the implications it had for the Second Coming. What further evidence was needed? God was indeed busily engaged in His grand purpose of restoring both Israel and the Church to their 1st-century points of departure.

The Influence of Periodicals

Several periodicals profoundly influenced Pentecostals concerning Zionism and the Jewish people. Among those most extensively read was the *Christian Evangel*, edited by Joseph and Alice Flower. They changed its name in 1915 to the *Weekly Evangel*. Flower became one of the founders of the Assemblies of God in 1914. He was the chief architect of the fourteenth article of the 1927 General Council of the Assemblies of God constitution's "Statement of Faith" which anticipated "the salvation of national Israel." No other 20th-century Christian denomination had such a clause in its basic system of faith.

Other Pentecostal publications included *Word and Witness*, edited by E.N. Bell from 1912–1915; *Word and Work*, edited by S.G. Otis and published from 1899 to 1940 for the sole purpose of spreading the good news of the Second Coming; Chicago's Stone Church published the *Latter Rain Evangel* from 1908 to 1939 when the Depression forced it to discontinue. It had a profound impact on Pentecostals everywhere. Among its many contributions was its focus on "the salvation of National Israel."

PENTECOSTAL APPRECIATION OF ZIONIST FEVER

Pentecostals like William MacArthur had expressed their highest regard for Theodor Herzl. Albert Weaver, in 1905, attended the Zionist conference in Basle, Switzerland, at which he heard heated discussion of the future habitation of the Jewish people. In 1909 he reported that some 30 Jewish settlements had been created in the Holy Land. The Turkish Sultan's new constitution permitted Jewish people to purchase land, and they lost no time buying up property north of Jerusalem. To Christian enthusiasts, these signs meant the Church Age was closing and the Kingdom Age was coming.[31]

In 1915, E.N. Bell, first General Chairman of the Assemblies of God, wrote of preparations for the return of the Jewish people to Palestine. He noted that Zionists were having difficulty soliciting the energies of the greater majority of the Jewish people. But Jewish voices were demanding respect and recognition in the first national Zionist gathering in Boston, Massachusetts, in 1915. Zionists purposed to give Jewish people their civic rights to freedom wherever they desired to live. Such coveted freedom would undoubtedly become reality at the end of World War I.[32]

In 1917, some 500 delegates at a New York demonstration demanded a Jewish republic in Palestine. The *Latter Rain Evangel* printed this in full.[33] The same year, the *Weekly Evangel* indicated that for every 100 Jewish people migrating to the Holy Land, thousands of Turks were migrating to America—proving God was providing homes for the Jewish people.[34] Meanwhile, the Sea of Galilee was full of fish, the Dead Sea was filled with chemicals useful to industry, and railways were being built in Palestine. All this was preparation for the Jewish return to the Promised Land. Albert Weaver suggested that Jewish allurement to other lands was nothing less than satanic opposition to God's will.

A prominent article in the 1915 *Weekly Evangel* told how New York rabbis called for American Jewish people to fast on Mondays and pray for the end of the European war as millions of Jewish people were presently being persecuted. E.N. Bell, in Word and Witness in the same year, quoted descriptions of current Jewish sufferings in Europe and told how 200 pogroms (violent attacks) had occurred in Poland since the beginning of the war in 1914. The 1916 *Latter Rain Evangel* depicted horrific descriptions of the suffering and death of some 7,000 Jewish people in Austria. Jewish people were also suffering appalling Turkish abuse. The governor vowed the Jewish people would suffer the genocidal Armenian fate.[35] Yet, along with legal Jewish acquisition of land

and the creation of 100 Jewish schools, the rapid construction of hospitals, homes, and synagogues, were all celebrated. Surely the Jewish people would live in freedom at the conclusion of the European war.

Alexander A. Boddy (1854–1930), world traveler, academic revivalist, and British Pentecostal pioneer, confidently expected that Britain's king would reward the 50,000 Jewish people serving in his army by giving them a new position of freedom and equality not known since the Temple's destruction in a.d. 70. The regathering of Israel would include inheriting the land biblically promised to Abraham from the Nile to the Euphrates.

The key composers of early Pentecostalism anticipated a Pentecostal Jewish world in fulfillment of Bible prophecy. Charles Parham believed the sealed witnesses of Revelation 7 would be Israelites sealed with the Holy Spirit as accompanied by speaking in tongues. Embracing the Scripture that "the Jew requires a sign," Pentecostals envisioned new Messianic faith rising in Israel as "signs, wonders, and miracles" occurred by Pentecostal activities in Zion.

William MacArthur insisted that many bright minds in Israel were expecting the Jewish embrace of Jesus. Pentecostals had "every encouragement to be faithful to the Great Commission to give the gospel to the Jew first." He saw Israel's spiritual transformation as foundational to the successful evangelization of the pagan world. As a foretaste to this, many in Israel had already come to faith in Christ, and Jewish people the world over were reading Hebrew copies of the New Testament.

William H. Cossum also encouraged Pentecostal evangelism among the Jewish people. All abuse of Jewish people must end. The Pentecostal experience would be poured out on a redeemed national Israel in greater measure than in Acts 2. Israel was, in fact, the key to the right understanding of Pentecost. When Israel would flow in Pentecostal power, global evangelization would be successfully completed. Meanwhile, Christians should maintain a loving heart for the salvation of Israel in anticipation of Israel's national redemption.

PENTECOSTALS AND GLOBAL MISSIONS

According to Paul Boyer, American historian at the University of Wisconsin, in his *When Time Shall be No More*, Evangelicals greeted World War I with millennial expectation. A flood of books, pamphlets, and articles heralded the end of the present age in the light of prophecy. By the end of the war, many Evangelicals, including some Pentecostals, were prepared to accept the end of civilization. Yet most Pentecostals had a positive spirit. They focused on the soon establishment of a Zionist state and the Second Coming.

From their beginnings, Pentecostals felt a powerful call to action. Messages through prophetic gifts encouraged urgent evangelistic activity. Their sense of destiny encouraged spiritual warfare in foreign missions and proliferation of congregations in both major cities and small towns. Soon some were saying one could go anywhere and find three things: Coca-Cola, Singer sewing machines, and the Assemblies of God.

It was a profound shock to early Pentecostals after a few years that the world was not rapidly and fully evangelized as they expected. Yet in spite of Pentecostal naiveté, the Pentecostal mission enterprise quickly became universal. It soon surpassed the effectiveness of many older mission societies.

PENTECOSTAL PARTICIPATION
IN MISSION TO ISRAEL

Pentecostal evangelism among Jewish people had a unique significance. Their missionaries proclaimed both growing numbers of Jewish people coming to salvation in Jesus and the vitality of the Spirit in Jewish ministries. In 1904, Hebrew Christian Bernhard Angel wrote that the Spirit of God was at work among Israel. Materialism and rationalism were proving disastrous to Jewish religion, yet prejudice was breaking down. The New York Jewish community had its own remnant studying the Gospel. Jewish people, convinced by the activities of the Holy Spirit, were leading others in worship. Angel himself was the regular Saturday preacher to 100 Jewish people. Some 120 societies with 850 workers were spending a million dollars annually for global Jewish evangelism. Hundreds of Jewish people were preaching the Gospel they once despised.[36]

J.R. Flower's *The Pentecost* regularly expressed support for Jewish evangelism and the salvation of national Israel. He regularly included testimonies of missionary work among the Jewish people. Louie Schneiderman testified that London had seven Jewish missions and many Jewish missionaries.[37] John G. Lake, famous Pentecostal healing evangelist, reported some 200-300 Jewish people in attendance at every service in his South African services.[38] Flower also called on Pentecostals to believe for miracles in conjunction with the salvation of the Jewish people.

Albert Weaver insisted in 1909 that Pentecostals owed a great debt to the Jewish people for the Gospel. It was their Christian sacred duty to give the Gospel in return to the Jewish people. To illustrate Jewish spiritual hunger for the Truth, Weaver indicated he knew a rabbi who neither ate nor slept till he finished reading the New Testament and then became an ardent Christian.

In 1910, the *Latter Rain Evangel* published a seven-page testimony of Maurice Ruben, a Jewish believer living in Pittsburgh. His spiritual transformation entirely changed his life. He lost his wife and son as a result of it, but was later reconciled when his wife became a believer. Together they shared the Gospel with Jewish people of Pittsburgh. Already more than 200 Jewish people had accepted Christ. Some of these new Jewish believers went into Jewish evangelism in spite of bitter official Jewish opposition.

The next year the same magazine highlighted Phillip Sidersky's Pentecostal Jewish mission in Baltimore. His recent Yom Kippur services had attracted over 1,000 Jewish adults. He gave them Yiddish New Testaments and tracts after the services. A year later, the dramatic testimony of Jewish believer and son of Berlin rabbi Joseph Lewek was published. After suffering religious persecution in Germany, he made a difficult transition to America. Here he was ultimately spiritually redeemed and called to the Christian ministry.[39]

Alex A. Boddy endorsed a number of Jewish ministries including that of businessman William Bernard of Liverpool, Bernard's Jewish disciple Paul in Poland, and Otto Kaper in Silesia. Boddy also pointed to the missionary activities in Jerusalem of Elizabeth Brown and Dr. Frances Murcutt. Murcutt encountered intense hatred, but this helped her realize that only prayer and faith would accomplish the work.[40] Boddy also reported that the 1913 Sunderland Convention emphasized that the English had missionary duties to both Jewish people and Gentiles.[41]

E.N. Bell's enthusiasm for the revival of the Jewish nation caused him to print 1913 and 1914 newsletters from A.J. Benson of New York, who wrote that Christians needed to give Jewish people the pure Gospel. He complained of anti-missionary efforts of young Jewish people. But since the heavenly host is with the missionaries, prayers assured him of victory.[42]

Missionary Sarah Smith told of Pentecost falling in the German colony of Jerusalem, with speaking in tongues as in Acts 2:4.[43] Charles Leonard, Mary Smithson, and Florence Bush were doing orphanage and pastoral work in Jerusalem. But Pentecostal Jewish mission efforts in Israel were largely unnoticed by the non-Pentecostal world.

By 1916, Florence Bush moved her missionary work to Cleveland's 65,000 Jewish people. Persecution commenced in the spring when rabbis condemned her in a Jewish newspaper. But this resulted in increased Jewish attendance. By summer, seven Jewish people rejoiced in Jesus, prepared for water baptism, and were seeking Spirit-baptism.[44]

Charles Spellman, a lesser-known Jewish missionary, moved from Jerusalem to Los Angeles, opening a Jewish ministry at Bethel Temple. Alberta Boothby and her husband ministered in Jerusalem and Egypt for nine years. They shared their faith in Jewish wards in hospitals and witnessed in five socialist Jewish colonies. Several Jewish people, including a rabbi and a few Jewish youths, came to faith in Jesus after studying Messianic prophecies with the Boothbys.[45]

Phillip Sidersky, Jewish missionary of Baltimore, said Spirit-filled Jewish believers were needed to present the pure Gospel of grace to bring Jewish people to accept Jesus as their Messiah. He proclaimed the greatest Jewish need is Jesus since all Jewish aspirations will find their ultimate fulfillment in Him.[46]

Alex A. Boddy recounted dramatic victories of Jewish Pentecostal spiritual transformation in *Confidence* to inspire belief that proper demonstration of the Holy Spirit's power would bring Jewish people to Pentecostal faith. In 1913, he wrote of the spiritual transformation of a young Jewish assistant to the local rabbi. The young man visited a Pentecostal service where he received a message from God through the Hebrew tongues-speaking of a Gentile. The young man was baptized in the Holy Spirit with speaking in tongues that night. Well-known Pentecostals were named as witnesses to this.[47]

Jewish participation in the Pentecostal experience was vital to Pentecostalism's restorationism, the return of the Church to its pristine 1st-century sanctification, and empowerment for its global mission. Jewish partnership in God's fraternal twin restorations of both Israel and the Church confirmed the very essence of Pentecostal teaching. That Jewish people coming to faith in Jesus strengthened the Pentecostal witness.

FORMATION OF THE GENERAL COUNCIL OF THE ASSEMBLIES OF GOD

The Assemblies of God organized over April 2-12, 1914, in Hot Springs, Arkansas. The central theme was the expectation of the Second Coming. But the experience of speaking in tongues provided the basis for their organization. They emphasized that they were creating a New Testament Church fellowship. They would encourage religious spontaneity and freedom of worship as they sought the guidance of the Holy Spirit.[48] They adopted no creed or confession of faith at this meeting. Yet by 1916, they did officially adopt a statement of "Fundamental Truths" that included tongues as the "initial physical sign" of baptism in the Holy Spirit.

Most Pentecostal leaders at the time were fiercely independent restoration-ists and opposed religious organization beyond the local pastoral level. The wholesome Pentecostal promises of inner peace, healing, heavenly provision, dignity, and family of God status were attractive indeed to leaders and com-munities alike.[49]

The Assemblies of God found their greatest numerical strength in the greater Ozark region of the Midwest. They stood ready to perpetuate fun-damentalist, puritanical, and emotionally revivalistic patterns that were dying away in many other Christian circles. An Assemblies of God reading course and Bible school curriculum included the works of Moody, Torrey, Simpson, Murray, and Pierson. Scofield's Reference Bible was also used. Keswick teach-ing of enduement of power by the Holy Spirit dominated Pentecostal thought.

Two crucial points in the 1916 "Statement of Fundamental Truths" cen-tered on the baptism of the Holy Spirit and Millennialism. At the same time, they began distancing themselves from those prone to new revelations and stubborn independence.[50]

By 1917, the Assemblies of God included 620 ministers, 73 mission-aries, and about 75,000 adherents. But the early freedoms associated with divine immediacy, "heaven below" and readiness for all to be used as a divine mouthpiece were replaced with more conventional Evangelical boundaries. They reined in the pursuit of ever fresher revelations and ever greater apos-tolic anointings. They proclaimed the New Testament as all sufficient. They began to take history and the future into account. This would have far-reaching effects on the Pentecostal movement. But the Day of Pentecost in Acts 2 was still the Pentecostal model of Christian experience to be forever emulated.

Chapter 3

CLASSICAL PENTECOSTALISM'S ROMANTIC IDEOLOGY OF ZIONISM (1918–1945)

Many corners of society forced the Assemblies of God Pentecostals in 1914 to face hostility. Secular society was increasingly disapproving. Coping with it was manageable because religious leaders could explain the mocking rejection in terms of the godlessness of worldly opposition. But the harsh condemnation of Pentecostalism by closer religious groups and Christian peers was harder to understand and accept.

Many foes and even a few friends met the Pentecostal acceptance of glossolalia as the initial evidence of Spirit-baptism with ridicule and contempt. The Spirit-filled tongues speakers desperately needed a distinctive, a cause célèbre, to justify their ongoing independent existence.

As discussed in Chapter 2, the Bible's Latter Rain prophecies suggested a dual restoration of both Zion and the Church. Pentecostals had seized on fraternal restoration to legitimize their experience and their expectation of restoration and revitalization of Christianity for the purposes of regaining proper Church spiritual form as in the Book of Acts. The Hebrew Bible's Latter Rain prophecies centered on biblical Israel. Pentecostals needed to believe in God's ongoing activity with Israel in time and space. Any allegorical substitution of the Church for Israel was thus senseless. It was more pragmatic for Pentecostals to identify with a nationally restored Israel to establish their theme of a twin restoration. God was busily revitalizing both Israel and the Church to their 1st-century heritage. Pentecostals, especially the Assemblies of God, readily favored Zion from their earliest years. They demonstrated their sense of genuine compatibility with Zionism.

In this chapter we are examining carefully the Pentecostal relation to Zionism between 1918 and 1945. There was a high pitch of Pentecostal enthusiasm and passion for Zionist advances between World War I and the end of World War II. Pentecostal literature celebrated developments in Palestine and demonstrated a long-term devotion to Zionism's success.

Pentecostals viewed the restoration of Zion as the fulfillment of prophecy. Celebrating Zionism's hopeful message of national restoration afforded legitimacy to Pentecostalism in many ways. Since the Hebrew Bible's prophecies of Zion's rebuilding nearly always spoke of a corresponding Gentile spiritual component, it was relatively simple to capitalize on Zionism to help explain Pentecostal relevance to the last days.

Since Pentecostals had their own enemies in the Evangelical and Holiness camps who angrily disputed Pentecostal restorationist claims, they could appreciate the very real opposition the Zionists were likewise facing for what the Pentecostals considered Israel's biblically mandated cause. Pentecostal literature clearly sided with Zionism and defended it against Arab, British, and international opposition.

However, Pentecostals were not yet entirely cleansed of inherited anti-Semitism. Ante-Nicene Christianity (a.d. 100–325) saw both the gradual decline of apostolic miracles and the Church's embrace of supersession, e.g., the replacement of Israel by the Church. Many Pentecostals rapidly embraced restored apostolic manifestations but only more gradually came to understand the strategic role of a restored national Israel.

There was sporadic fascination with British-Israelism and a dispensationalist tendency to identify the future antichrist as Jewish. But the Assemblies of God worked to condemn such traces of anti-Semitism on biblical grounds.

The one difficulty for Pentecostals in their view of Zionism as fellow travelers and partners was the continued Jewish rejection of Christ. But Pentecostals consoled themselves by believing that the Jewish rejection of Christ was a temporary problem. It would soon be overcome, since Pentecostals felt the need to evangelize the Jewish people in anticipation of their return to Zion. First-century-styled apostolic Christianity would benefit the Jewish people since glossolalia represented the "strange tongues" that Isaiah 28:11 advised Jewish people to expect. The "tongues" people of Pentecostalism perceived themselves as having a unique contribution to make toward the revitalization of Israel.

IDEOLOGICAL CHANGES
IN AMERICAN PENTECOSTALISM

The general shift in American Pentecostal thinking in the period from 1918 to 1945 had a direct bearing on the Pentecostal romance with Zionism. An overview of Pentecostal circumstances and worldview as it modified during this period can yield appreciation of their compulsion to cling to Zionism. They did this in spite of world events and occasional internal voices of protest.

Recent histories of American Pentecostalism by Edith Blumhofer, Vinson Synan, Grant Wacker, Robert Anderson, and Margaret Poloma have established the internal trends and historical movements of Pentecostals generally and the Assemblies of God in particular during this era. A window here and there on the Pentecostal worldview enables detection of their higher need for Zionism than that of either Evangelicalism or Fundamentalism.

World War I generated a new level on international awareness among all Americans. The aftermath of the 1917 Balfour Declaration and the establishment of the British Mandate electrified American Pentecostals—so did the successes of Zionist rebuilding in Palestine. Yet rising waves of anti-Semitic propaganda from Europe cooled small pockets of Pentecostalism for the short term.

Post-World-War I Pentecostals faced a new identity crisis that would lead to new actions. As early as 1908, a Pentecostal missionary training institute was operating in Alliance, Ohio. The Assemblies of God from their beginning saw the need and purpose to establish a school to train ministers and missionaries. To meet the need, they started Central Bible Institute in 1922 with a faculty that soon included a Jewish believer, Myer Pearlman, and graduates of the Christian and Missionary Alliance Bible School in Nyack, New York.

This was followed by a network of Bible institutes in the 1920s and 1930s. Some of their educators borrowed dispensational thought relegating Zion's victory to a millennial future. By this they sought to dampen Pentecostal romantic speculations on coming Zionist accomplishments. Many feared an extensive correlation between Pentecostalism and vulnerable Zionism might ultimately de-legitimize Pentecostalism. Yet even throughout the Depression and European Nazi years leading up to World War II, the indefatigable exuberance of Pentecostal enthusiasm for Zion continued. It challenged and checked those more committed to denominational self-interest.

The magnetic pull to the National Association of Evangelicals in the early 1940s overwhelmed conventional Pentecostal reservations against social and political entanglements. It also compelled them to modify earlier teachings to gain greater social acceptance. They still condemned all forms of anti-Semitism. Yet during the 1930s and 1940s, the Assemblies of God increasingly balanced its expressions of Zionist support with frequent "soft-pedaled" distancing from it.

Until 1918, Pentecostals viewed social, political, and intellectual transitions through the grid of biblical prophecy. Everything appeared to point to the Second Coming. Postwar "pilgrims and strangers" needed to take sides on cultural matters because they stood "on the firing line" for God. They were no longer quite as alienated from American society as their earlier millenarian restorationism mandated.[1] So they interpreted World War I to be an extension of the spiritual warfare they were forever engaged in. They would be "in the world" but not "of the world."

Charles Parham taught that glossolalia was primarily given for Gospel proclamation in all languages. Pentecostals needed to legitimate speaking in tongues as the initial evidence of Spirit baptism. This motivated them to take a definitive position. They recognized human limitations to affect full apostolic renewal. But they proclaimed that Latter Rain restoration was indeed well underway. However, the Second Coming had been divinely postponed. The Latter Rain generation needed to relate to an earth-bound future after all. To some measure they relaxed the immanence of their millenarianism and restorationism. Rather, they emphasized the "fullness" of the Pentecostal gospel—that is, Fundamentalism with tongues.[2]

As Pentecostals pondered their relationship with society for the next generation, new understandings emerged. They gave attention to citizenship, community, education, global missions, and the priority of spreading the Pentecostal message. The delay of the Second Coming plainly mandated a modified explanation for the utility of speaking in tongues.[3]

Assemblies of God constituents assumed a fundamentalist identity, but remained somewhat oblivious to the theological problems that came with it. They were more prepared to pursue relations with other "born-again" Evangelicals. While some Pentecostals had insisted that their tongues experience was vital to the new birth experience, the Assemblies of God believed the new birth and Spirit baptism experiences were distinct. Although Pentecostal theology was incompatible with strict dispensationalist fundamentalism, most were able to hold the two opposing systems of thought in tension with minor difficulty. Even while Fundamentalists were hostile to what they called Pentecostal "error," the Assemblies of God adherents gladly related to Fundamentalism's emphases on biblical inerrancy and the current fulfillment of prophecy.[4]

The World's Christian Fundamentals Association, organized in 1919, severely condemned Pentecostalism in their 1928 convention, calling it a menace.[5] Fundamentalists accepted Scofield's dispensationalism, which regarded tongues speaking and divine healing as characteristic of the New Testament apostolic period alone. Their purpose was to introduce the dispensation of grace or the Church Age in the 1st century. According to this system of thought, God discontinued both tongues and healings at the inauguration of the Church Age. Therefore, they regarded Pentecostals as cultic. Methodists and other Evangelicals discredited Pentecostals as frauds or worse.

By the second and third generation, Pentecostals largely ascended to the middle class socially and economically. The emotionalism, informality, working lay clergy, millennialism, and holiness standards of Pentecostalism appealed to myriads of hard-working Americans.[6] At the same time, they labored to become more financially viable. It also seemed that as Assemblies of God constituents achieved greater social stability and circumstance, their Pentecostal experiences lessened. Improved social conditions led to the relaxation of their need for such experience. The precise meaning of Spirit baptism was changing among them. Doctrinal orthodoxy slowly replaced enthusiastic spiritual experiences. This brought Pentecostals ever closer to identification with Evangelicals.[7]

Early Pentecostals advocated social aloofness from an American culture perceived as God-defiant. Christians who were friendly with the world were backsliders bent on negating holy and Spirit-filled living. American individualism nourished this Pentecostal independence from society. But with their post-World War I greater economic status and social immersion into mainstream American culture, Pentecostals resolved to become engaged in the world about them. For example, the Assemblies of God moved away from its deep suspicion of patriotism and its advocacy of conscientious objection to military involvement. Few Pentecostals engaged in armed services in World War I. But by World War II, the Assemblies of God strongly endorsed both patriotism and military service.

Between the wars, the Latter Rain emphasis was moderated. The Pentecostals were increasingly accepted by the Evangelical mainstream as evidenced by their invitation to join the newly formed National Association of Evangelicals in 1941. Soon they resorted to historical records to substantiate their claims of continuous Pentecostal apostolic anointing from the Book of Acts to the present. Yet the modern link to 1st-century Pentecostalism remained strong, as reflected in the first histories of modern Pentecostalism by P.C. Nelson (1940) and Klaude Kendrick (1959). They connected the Assemblies of God directly to the Book of Acts.

Pentecostals wanted to disassociate from an ecclesiastical history contaminated by its official condemnation of continued apostolic activity—a history full of idolatrous clerical embellishment. They wanted to demonstrate historically that God's will had always been the continued apostolic Church. Pentecostalism was new to modern Christianity, but there had been ongoing pockets or periodic outbreaks of charismatic experience. Pentecostal experience was always the will of God for the Church.

Pentecostals believed they had no connection to the Church's historical guilt. They had now prophetically risen to condemn the historical ecclesiastical system. So they asserted their own historical respectability as the persecuted faithful remnant through the centuries. One reality did keep most Pentecostals in step with their earlier stress on Christ's return. They continued to hope for the national rebirth of Israel in Zion. Some might challenge other signs of the times as periodically recurrent in history. But the Zionist hope to establish a Jewish national homeland in Palestine provided Pentecostals with a final link with restorationism. It would underscore the legitimacy of the Latter Rain Pentecostal identity. If the Jewish people had abandoned Zionism, it would have undermined the Latter Rain teaching and the very legitimacy of Pentecostal restorationism.

As Zionism continued to build international momentum, Pentecostals took greater hope for the climax of the age, Christ's Second Coming. They saw Zionism as a direct contemporary witness to Latter Rain phenomena, including speaking in tongues as the initial evidence of Spirit baptism. The initial evidence theme, in turn, provided legitimacy for the perpetuation of Pentecostalism. Thus, Zionism strongly seconded the Pentecostal position.

Before the 1920s, Pentecostals could hardly conceive of a delayed Second Coming. After that, however, it became increasingly apparent that they needed educational institutions to equip young preachers for tomorrow's expansion. They soon realized that they needed to found their own Bible schools and colleges since most denominational schools were openly hostile to Pentecostals.[8] Some feared that Pentecostal schools would compromise Pentecostal dynamism and identity. But many called for a new understanding of the contemporary reality to revitalize Pentecostalism in the light of the delay of Christ's return.

Most Assemblies of God pastors and educators in the 1920s had very little formal education themselves. As restoration themes and expectations slipped, some recognized the need for quality education of youth to carry the torch to the next generation. Emphasis in the Assemblies of God gradually shifted to the long-term perpetuation of Pentecostalism for the 20th century. The function of speaking in tongues was viewed increasingly as vital for the revival of one's own soul—by the edification mentioned in First Corinthians 14:4.

Pentecostalism still generally abstained from social involvement. They castigated those involved in the liberal "social gospel." Some thought taking care of the poor, hungry, and infirm victims of society gave them false hope. They believed social problems were, in fact, a fulfillment of biblical prophecy and should be left to play themselves out. Their focus remained on individual escape from eternal judgment while the world about them sunk deeper into the abyss. Others, however, did sponsor rescue missions for the poor.

Pentecostals overcame factionalism through step-by-step creation of official doctrinal positions and codes of conduct. The very features of denominationalism they once condemned now became standard practices in the Assemblies of God. Each new issue, heresy, or dilemma needed an appropriate response.

Until the 1940s, the Assemblies of God constituents were suspicious of any cooperation with non-Pentecostals. They rejected any thought of ecumenism or affiliation with other organizations. They believed they enjoyed fuller understanding of the biblical revelation than those who ignored the Holy Spirit's enlightenment and manifestations via the gifts. Thus, when the Assemblies of God cooperated with the National Association of Evangelicals in the 1940s, this separated them from more radical Pentecostals. Over time, some Pentecostals lost sight of their healing and tongues distinctives, making them more palatable to Evangelicals.

By participating in the National Association of Evangelicals, the Assemblies of God renewed its public commitment to revitalize America and evangelize the world. They continued to affirm apostolic power for the present age, but celebrated their affinity with Evangelicals on basically all other matters. This created new distance from other Pentecostals, but facilitated Pentecostal denominational responses toward Evangelical overtures in coming years. Many Assemblies of God leaders wanted to participate in what they considered the national chosenness of America and its God-given destiny.[9]

PENTECOSTAL PASSION FOR ZIONISM

Pentecostals had a deep-seated conviction of God's own hand in modern Zionism. They likewise felt an obligation to protest all forms of anti-Semitism. Thus, their romantic enthusiasm for Zionist objectives only escalated through both World Wars.

The Weekly Evangel reported in 1918 on a London Zionist demonstration of thanks to the British government for adopting the Balfour Declaration. Most of London's Jewish people favored a proposed national home in Palestine. They responded emotionally to the Hebrew words for "Next Year in Jerusalem," a phrase traditionally spoken by all each year at the conclusion of the Passover celebration. This brought hallelujahs to Pentecostals. God would be using Jewish leaders as He had Ezra and Nehemiah.[10]

In 1924 the *Pentecostal Evangel* included a report that recent congressional legislation aided European Jewish people in their return to Zion, and a New York rabbi had offered assurances that a temple like Solomon's would be rebuilt in Jerusalem.[11]

Frank M. Boyd, Assemblies of God theologian and educator, recounted in 1925 the dramatic story of Theodor Herzl and Zionism. The Jewish national spirit was already regenerated, and hope for a national home in Palestine was generating altruistic efforts among Jewish people and many others. Boyd celebrated the influx of Jewish immigrants and gave glowing statistics of Zion's agricultural exports to the West. With passion, Boyd recounted Eliezer Ben Yehuda's successful struggle to revive spoken Hebrew. He was enthusiastic about the new Hebrew University on Mount Scopus, overlooking Jerusalem on the east. Jewish activities in all directions were accomplishing wonders.[12]

Myer Pearlman, a Hebrew Christian, as the 1925 commencement speaker at Central Bible Institute, told in shocking detail of Christian treatment of the Jewish people in the Middle Ages. But now things had dramatically changed. Hope existed for a national return to Palestine. This was no longer a far-off event. Pearlman went on to become an outstanding professor, theologian, and writer of Sunday school materials.

In 1927, Pearlman wrote that, without Palestine, the Jewish people had always recognized Israel to be incomplete. The Zionist movement now had been birthed out of a furnace of affliction, but it was now hoping to affect the Jewish return to Zion by political means.[13] Some, in fact, had gone so far as to consider Herzl a prophet.

When the *Pentecostal Evangel* published Chief Rabbi Kuk's message to the Jewish people, it contended that Kuk properly encouraged Zionists to cling to the promises of the Bible rather than rely on governments.[14] It also reported that agricultural colonists of "Peta Tikva" openly anticipated the coming of the Messiah. Kuk sounded the shofar on Mount David. What a day of marvels!

Jesus is coming![15] Thus, there was solid correlation between Zion's rebirth and Christ's return in Pentecostal thought.

The 1931 *Pentecostal Evangel* seemed eager to give Chaim Weizmann credit for rescuing civilization. This Jewish professor of chemistry in the University of Manchester, England, had invented TNT for which he was ultimately rewarded with the Balfour Declaration! In 1932, the same periodical ran an extensive column on Zionist developments. Jewish people had suffered exile when they preferred Caesar to Christ. But now God was stirring up Jewish people to go back to their land. In support of this, it quoted Nahum Sokolow, the president of the World Zionist Organization. He said that the Jewish people were coming to Palestine to stay. Threats and violence would not stop them. The same year, the *Pentecostal Evangel* expressed hope that Christian enthusiasm for Zionism would translate into Jewish evangelism.[16] Pentecostals perceived that Zionism without Israel's faith in Jesus was ultimately insufficient.

Myer Pearlman's *Knowing the Doctrines of the Bible*, published in 1937, became the standard theological textbook for training Assemblies of God clergy for the next generation. He described Christ as the promised Messiah of Israel. In discussing the founding of the Church in Jerusalem, he blurred any distinction between Israel and the Church. By this he linked Israel and the Church in perpetuity. Current distresses and the threat of World War he took as signs of the soon reestablishment of Jewish people in Zion. He also expected this would result in a spiritual resurrection of Israel.

PENTECOSTAL CELEBRATION OF DEVELOPMENTS IN ZION

Pentecostal publications expressed exuberant joy as they witnessed reconstruction of the Promised Land. Amazing Zionist accomplishments testified to the pending climax of salvation history. Staggering growth of the Jewish population, new Hebrew academies, the revival of Hebrew as a modern spoken language, and Jewish people desiring to restore the land to its former beauty, all made Pentecostals feel the legitimacy of their own restoration experiences. By 1936, Pentecostals reported that over a million Jewish people had returned to Zion. Songs of Jewish restoration reflected their burning hearts. Already they were turning Zion into a world class agricultural country.

Redemption of the Land

Restoration of the land further pointed to the last days. Altruistic efforts of Jewish youths were recreating a Garden of Eden in Zion. God had left treasures latent within the soils and seas of the Promised Land. Now they would be mined for Jewish national benefit. They believed the 1924 estimate of $40 billion in mineral wealth in the Dead Sea was a miracle of divine providence. God had preserved it for the benefit of the forthcoming Jewish nation.[17]

The building of modern cities like Tel Aviv exhilarated Pentecostals. They considered astonishing its mushrooming growth and industrialization. The Jewish people had set out to scientifically colonize Palestine, but God had supernaturally intervened. Annual increase in rain for 20 years had prepared the land for the return of Israel. The land was now "blossoming as the rose."

Amazing Jewish skills and sacrifices enabled extensive use of Haifa's port; the redemption of 40,000 acres of plague-infested swamps and 12,500 acres of malaria-infested swamps of the Hula plains were in process. Pentecostals believed Jewish people would soon own Samaria because God would most assuredly keep His Word. The 1937 *Pentecostal Evangel* sang the praises of these Jewish accomplishments because Palestine under the Arabs and Turks had deteriorated into a barren waste.[18] Pentecostals expected the renewed farming productivity would attract even more Jewish people to Zion.

Construction in the Cities of Zion

Pentecostals took Jewish return to Zion as a sign of Christ's coming. The spectacular rise of Tel Aviv assured Zion's future prosperity. New housing and massive construction in major cities, including Jerusalem and Haifa, were positive signs of the Second Coming of Christ.[19]

The *Pentecostal Evangel* reported the glories of Galilee. Tiberias was host to many natural springs where Imperial Roman baths had yielded valuable minerals and curative benefits. Tel Aviv's population, in its first 26 years after 1910, grew from 550 to 125,000. Jerusalem was being built up. Its beautiful neighborhoods saw property values increase by 1,000 percent. The fig tree had budded, and the Gentile era was closing.

Thanks to Jewish Tenacity and Skill

The *Pentecostal Evangel* considered the economic future of Palestine secure since it was in Jewish hands. But a 1928 article told of Zionist struggles from 1926 to 1928. Because Palestine was receiving more immigrants than it could absorb, a surprising number had returned to their former nations. Zionist's enemies wanted to assign failure to the cause. Yet between 1924 and 1944 world Jewry invested half a billion dollars in Zionist causes.[20] Jewish people in Zion refused to let widespread Arab violence discourage them. Pentecostals were quick to publish refutations of false charges of Jewish confiscation of Arab lands.[21]

The Ultimate Jewish Victory Scene

Pentecostals admitted that the supernatural restoration of the land had not yet led to Israel's national salvation in Christ. But they were assured that the Jewish return in unbelief would soon be mended as Jewish people returned to God through faith in Jesus. Jewish population growth was the beginning and would lead to the supernaturally desired climax. God had brought this growth for His own divine restoration agenda. That children were playing in the streets of Israel was fulfillment of biblical prophecy.[22] Reports of Jewish euphoria in Zion directly translated into Pentecostal euphoria in America.[23]

PENTECOSTAL IDEOLOGY OF ZIONISM
AS FULFILLED PROPHECY

Pentecostals published as early as 1918 that Israel is the true key to the philosophy of history. All history has been tailored to reposition the Jewish people in Zion. God-defiant nations had abused the Jewish people, but God would still make Israel His ambassador to the world.[24] After a season of divine chastening, a God-resistant Israel would come to messianic faith. The nations had never been able to consume the indigestible Jew. Like Jonah, the tattered but surviving prophet, the Jewish people would miraculously survive to perform their prophetic mission.

The *Pentecostal Evangel* declared in 1922 that Zionist efforts anticipated Jesus' reign over the restored kingdom of Israel.[25] Mark John Levy, a Jewish believer widely appreciated in the first decade of the Assemblies of God, published a tract in 1923 that spoke of Jewish restoration in the Holy Land as preparation for Christ's return and peace on earth.[26]

Pentecostals held two conflicting issues in tension. One was the Eternal God's commitment to Israel's perpetual inheritance. The other was the Jewish rejection of Jesus. The *Pentecostal Evangel* in 1925 said the Bible proves Israel could no more pass away than the Word of God itself. But shutting Israel's national eye to Jesus was a grave sin. It resulted in judgments on Israel foretold in Moses' Law. Yet God had determined thousands of years in the past that Palestine belonged to the Jewish people. Those unhappy with God's decree could not annul God's contract with Israel.

Frank Boyd, in 1925, stated that one of the most striking current developments was the plain evidence of God fulfilling His covenant promises to Israel. Only self-blinded people could miss what the Bible taught on Israel's restoration. Thirty years of Zionism had now prepared the way for God's restoration of Zion. In 1927, the *Pentecostal Evangel* again linked the Second Coming to the restoration of the Jewish nation in Zion. Israel was the key to both comings of Jesus.[27]

Pentecostals held in 1931 that recent outbreaks between Jewish people and Arabs were due to construction rivalry between mosque and temple advocates. Pentecostals recognized that Zionism was political rather than religious, and many decried that Zionists were oblivious to their fulfilling prophecy even while returning in unbelief. The Latter Rain Evangel in 1933 indicated that the return in unbelief was a temporary problem. Israel would soon return to the Lord and embrace faith in Jesus. Until then, however, unrepentant Jewish people would face woe and suffering.[28]

In spite of the obstacles, Zionist successes commended the Pentecostal belief in the restoration of all things. In 1934, the *Pentecostal Evangel* declared that the most striking sign of the times was a Palestine destined to play the most dramatic role of the endtimes, Second Coming, and the millennial age. Though many Jewish people had become egalitarian-focused Communists after centuries of international suffering, the survival of the Jewish people remained the "national miracle of the ages."[29] The return to Zion of the Jewish people on the heels of new persecutions by antichristic governments pointed to the return of the Messiah. Jesus will destroy all such evil powers and establish His Kingdom. In 1936, the *Pentecostal Evangel* reiterated these beliefs.[30]

Myer Pearlman understood the Jewish dilemma to be "spiritual dislocation." Satan was targeting the Jewish people for abuse since God had a wonderful destiny for Israel. Ironically, the nations Israel should have been preaching the Gospel to became the sources of much Jewish suffering.[31]

Most dispensationalists and many Pentecostals believed the antichrist would mastermind seven years of Jewish suffering. This made Jewish suffering still repugnant but more consistent with Evangelical expectation. One writer named Hitler as his nominee for antichrist. The antichrist's attacks upon the Jewish people would be the final stroke of chastening against Jewish apostasy. Christ Himself will defeat the armies of the antichrist and redeem Israel.[32]

Ernest S. Williams, general superintendent of the Assemblies of God, in a December 10, 1944, published Sunday school lesson discussed the Jewish people as God's chosen people. He described how the Jewish people have survived and claimed that every spiritual blessing that has come to other races came originally from the Jewish people. This is a fulfillment of God's promise to Abraham. Israel is still a special object of God's love. But Israel had not yet fulfilled her mission.[33]

AMERICAN PENTECOSTALISM'S IDEOLOGICAL REACTION TO ANTI-ZIONISM

The *Pentecostal Evangel* of 1931 reported that Hebrew Christians were dissatisfied with anything less than the spiritual regeneration of Israel. Also, a new generation of Zionists had become displeased with Chaim Weizmann's old style. They wanted more than a mere homeland. A Jewish state was needed.[34] But these nuances paled in contrast to Arab, British, and other international opposition to Zionism.

Arab Opposition

The 1920 Latter Rain Evangel labeled Arab uprisings against the Jewish people as the work of satan. So did Frank Boyd in 1925, though Boyd also laid heavy blame on the papacy and on Arab hatred of Western powers. The 1928 *Pentecostal Evangel* indicated that the Arab-Jewish conflict dated back to the biblical epic of Ishmael versus Isaac. Because this appeared to give the conflict a biblical cause, many Assemblies of God people seized on this and used it throughout the 20th century.

Arabs complained that Jewish immigration brought them economic woes. The *Pentecostal Evangel* in 1933 insisted that this was baseless propaganda. Figures had been exaggerated to negatively influence Jewish immigration policy. The Jewish people actually brought with them capital, energy, knowledge, and skills that stood to benefit the Arabs.[35]

Assemblies of God educational material taught that the highly relaxed Arab work ethic was no match for Jewish diligence. The Jewish people were effectively colonizing the land by generous legal purchase and hard work. The Jewish successes had brought Arab enmity. They promised to kill the Jewish people when the British left.[36] Arabs also destroyed Jewish wheat harvests, gardens, and orchards including 40,000 fruit trees. Yet Jewish people showed immense restraint, even at the cost of Jewish life.[37]

The new influx of Western Jewish capital weakened Arab powerbrokers' control and increased resentment against the Jewish newcomers. But in 1937, the *Pentecostal Evangel* reported that no Arab land came into Jewish hands without Arabs voluntarily selling at high prices.

British Opposition

When political crises generated Jewish agony, Pentecostal leaders did not challenge their own people to write the president or their senators. They called upon them rather to pray for the peace of Jerusalem. They believed such prayers would defeat the current British opposition to the Zionist cause.

Confidence in 1923 told how the British Bishop of Jerusalem preached in Durham Cathedral against Zionism. He said the Jewish people had done untold political harm to the Arabs. He protested that Zionism showed no interest in Judaism, so there was little hope of communicating the Gospel to the regathered Jewish people. But the *Pentecostal Evangel* answered British skepticism of Zionism by assuring that even if Zionism failed, God's purpose for Israel was divinely placed in the Jewish breast. Nothing could hinder the coming of a blessed summer for the Lord's ancient people.[38]

In 1930, the *Pentecostal Evangel* reported vociferous protests against British backpedaling on its earlier commitments to a Jewish national homeland. The British were severely limiting Jewish migration to Palestine and restricting land acquisition. In a December issue, the editor appealed for prayer as more effective than mass political gatherings. God would yet fulfill His purpose for Israel.[39]

British Jewish leader Lord Mechett, passionately urged the British to abide by the terms of the 1917 Balfour Declaration. His fiery speech ignited Pentecostal pulpits across America. Pentecostals welcomed the Jewish resolve to boldly rebuild Zion. They understood this as a fulfillment of prophecy and a sign of Christ's soon return.

Both Jewish people and Arabs disapproved of the British rationale for dividing the land. The *Pentecostal Evangel* indicted the British in 1945 for breaking covenant with Israel on the commitments of the Balfour Declaration. Soon the British, Hitler, Mussolini, and anti-Semites would "cry to the rocks to fall on them and cover them from the wrath of the One sitting on the throne" (see Rev. 6:16).[40]

International Opposition

The horrific events of World War II and the Jewish dilemma leading up to it compelled the Assemblies of God to constantly address the current international Jewish predicament. They did this with a set of Pentecostal resolutions: a Jewish national home in Zion, Jewish repentance and acceptance of Jesus as their Messiah, the Second Coming, and the establishment of Christ's millennial reign.

A news clip in 1919 told of 1.5 million Russian and Polish Jewish people in miles-long caravans traveling to Palestine. They could no longer endure the persecution and massacres in the lands of their birth. These included old men and women under heavy burdens, children, young husbands, and mothers carrying tiny babies in their arms.[41]

In 1930, the *Pentecostal Evangel* reported on world media focus on the 1929 massacres of the Jewish people.[42] In 1932, it told how Dr. Tannebaum at the American Jewish Congress said that the goal of European anti-Semitism was the complete destruction of the Jewish people.[43] The real solution would be a national regathering to the Shepherd of Israel. Political leaders such as Pharaoh, Haman, and Hitler had wanted to eliminate Jewish people to advance their own agendas. People have attempted to rid their societies of Jewish people by eradication or segregation. Segregation was either hostile (ghettoed Jewish existence) or friendly (embracing Zionism). But friendship with the Zionist aspiration is consistent with Scripture and will be accomplished by the Lord Himself.[44]

The *Pentecostal Evangel* also rehearsed Hitler's sinister rise to power and his hostility to the Jewish people. Hitler was making a huge mistake since God's Chosen People cannot be destroyed. In the spirit of antichrist, Hitler was replacing the Hebrew Bible with German mythology and seeking to compel Protestantism to come under his authority.

Anti-Semitism was commercially self-destructive. German confiscation of Jewish businesses and their placement into Aryan hands led to an 80 percent business failure rate. God would eliminate anti-Semites for their mistreatment of Jewish people. All who disobey God will suffer.[45]

PENTECOSTAL IDEOLOGICAL ENCOUNTER WITH ANTI-SEMITISM

From their earliest years, American Pentecostalism identified with Zionist developments in Palestine. After commencing in such a fashion, many were stunned by the blatant expressions of anti-Semitism surfacing from the 1920s with Henry Ford, European Nazism, and even in some corners of Pentecostalism. But many Pentecostals saw this as of satanic origin and felt it their duty to confront expressions of anti-Semitism with wholehearted condemnation.

Henry Ford and the Elders of Zion

A 1921 issue of *Confidence* was the first of Pentecostal literature to identify the anti-Semitism of Henry Ford, the American automobile manufacturer. It warned Pentecostals of Ford's 230-page book, *The International Jew, the World's Foremost Problem.* Ford stated that Jewish people were gaining power over the nations and the future of the planet. Ford even warned Christian prophecy teachers to beware.[46]

The same year, the *Pentecostal Evangel* boldly confronted Ford's anti-Semitism, stating he was a modern Balak. It was sure his effort would only yield a curse on him. God already viewed the Jewish people as returned to Zion. Ford would do well to repent and himself receive the Messiah Jesus.[47]

Myer Pearlman considered all persecution of Jewish people inspired and energized by satan. Unbelieving Gentiles might engage in anti-Semitic evil, but God had never commissioned biblical Christians to contribute to the sufferings of "the Wandering" Jewish people.[48]

Otto Klink offered Assemblies of God youth a general scoffing of anti-Semitism in 1935. He followed it with a disclaimer that he was only seeing this as a sign of the times, not as politics. He was aware of Pentecostal suspicion of participation in political affairs. Dependence on government could only bring disappointment. It was far nobler for citizens of God's Kingdom to rely solely on Providence for intervention in international politics. Meanwhile, many Jewish people could not pay the prohibitive ransoms required for them to leave Germany. Ardent Nazi pastors were rewriting the Bible to harmonize it with their anti-Jewish feelings. Assaults and murders of Jewish people made it seem that "Jacob's trouble" was near.[49]

In 1941, E.S. Williams recognized that an epidemic of anti-Semitism was sweeping over Europe. Vestiges of it were sweeping over Christendom. Even in America it was at an unprecedented level. He chided certain Pentecostal clergy saying that some Christian ministers would like to inflame Christians against the Jewish people.[50]

THE PENTECOSTAL CASE FOR ANTI-ZIONISM

There were few highly profiled incidents of anti-Zionism in the Pentecostal press. Yet Stanley Frodsham, who became editor of the *Pentecostal Evangel* in

1921, figured largely in the most damaging ones. He was temporarily influenced by the fictional *Protocols of the Elders of Zion*. He endorsed its general notions and tied together Jewish people, Bolsheviks, international conspiracy, and Zion. He would later regret this and publicly apologize in the 1930s.[51]

Frodsham's second mistake was his April 1922 cover article, "The Budding Fig Tree." It attacked Jewish efforts to restore Zion prior to Jewish national acknowledgment of Jesus and the Second Coming. God would not restore Israel until the world was successfully evangelized. Israel was trying to restore herself out of God's timing. All such efforts were doomed to fail. Israel must honor Deuteronomy 18:15-18 that promised another prophet like Moses. Until they resolved to obey the Mosaic Messiah Jesus, Jewish people would continue to suffer. But those who persecuted Jewish people would in turn be punished.[52]

PENTECOSTAL IDEOLOGICAL ENCOUNTER WITH BRITISH-ISRAELISM

For centuries, vestiges of Anglo identification with biblical Israel lingered in Christian circles. The more extreme version claimed that all of British ancestry was physical descendants of the Ten Lost Tribes of ancient Israel. God's covenant promises to Israel would be fully experienced as England and America executed the biblical mission of Israel in the end of the age.

To help alleviate confusion in many Pentecostal circles, the 1934 *Latter Rain Evangel* exposed the fallacies of British-Israelism. This was important, for this, like other replacement ideologies, could diminish Pentecostal affinity with the Jewish people. In the same magazine in 1936, Daniel Finestone, a Hebrew Christian, dismantled the basic tenets of British-Israelism. Others denounced it as a pernicious, dangerous delusion.[53]

Actually, the Ten Tribes were never lost. History shows that many of them joined with the later Jewish returnees after the times of Ezra and Nehemiah.

Some who had been left after 586 B.C. intermarried and became Samaritans. But the New Testament speaks of Anna, the prophetess who greeted the baby Jesus, as of the tribe of Asher, one of the ten tribes. Paul speaks of *"our twelve tribes"* (Acts 26:7). James wrote to the twelve tribes of Israel (see James 1:1). Paul knew which tribe he belonged to. So did the other Jewish people of his day. Today's Jewish people undoubtedly include members who are descendents from all twelve tribes.

THE JEWISH ANTICHRIST

Dispensationalists consistently held that the antichrist would be Jewish. In 1931, Nathan Beskin, a Hebrew Christian, challenged this belief and insisted the antichrist would not be Jewish.[54] But Myer Pearlman wrote that the origin and nationality of the antichrist were still matters of debate.[55]

Chapter 4

PENTECOSTAL IDEOLOGICAL CONDEMNATION OF ANTI-SEMITISM

Centuries of extra-biblical dogmatists were deeply implanted in the inherited portions of Pentecostal ideology. Yet they still sensed a duty toward the people of Israel. Pentecostal rationale for condemning anti-Semitism and treating Jewish people properly came from the Bible which gave them a legitimate understanding of this divine dictate and sound principle.

Pentecostals recognized Christians owed a grand debt of thanksgiving to the Jewish people. Revealed religion was given to humankind through them: the Bible, Christ, the Gospel, the apostles, and all that is precious to Christians. Christ came to save Israel, and God was not finished with them by a long shot.[1]

In 1937, Pentecostals chided any form of Christian anti-Semitism. The whole of Scripture testified to God's love for Israel. Those truly filled with the Spirit would love and pray for them.[2] They needed to share Paul's goodwill toward Israel and his hope for their salvation. Looking down on the Jewish people had been the Roman Church's transgression. The world had many proposed solutions to the "Jewish problem." God had the one real answer: the Jewish people in Zion with Jesus as King.

Pentecostals in 1934 saw growing anti-Semitism in America and Europe as pointing to Palestine as the only real hope for Jewish security and permanency. This was based on biblical passages from both Testaments that predicted Israel's restoration. These prophecies were conjoined with the Scriptural hope of Christ's return.[3] Some likened the Jew to the reluctant prophet Jonah. Even Peter's 3,000 new believers on the Day of Pentecost were only a handful compared to Nineveh's awakening. But when God succeeded in getting the Jewish people preaching the Gospel to the nations, the universe would witness the ultimate revival, the greatest in all human history.[4]

ANTI-SEMITISM AS AN
ALIEN INSTRUMENT FOR EVIL

All the peoples around Israel in ancient times were later scattered, assimilated, and lost their identity. Pentecostals recognized that the fact this did not happen to the Jewish people was a miracle of God. His present punishment of Jewish disobedience to the God-appointed, anointed King of Israel would soon terminate. God would avenge wrongs done to the Jewish people as the Bible promised. Myer Pearlman noted in 1932, with trepidation and anguish, the rising influence of Hitler in Germany and new laws against Jewish immigrants. Abuse of Jewish people would certainly result in German national decline.[5] Pentecostals called for proper treatment of the Jewish people, warning that nations that persecuted Jewish people had to pay for it. Jewish-abusing Czars in Russia had learned this the hard way.

Anti-Semites spread the *Protocols* again and declared the Jewish people had manipulated the depression. Nathan Beskin stated there was not a particle of evidence to suggest the *Protocols* had any legitimacy.[6] Pentecostals attacked the *Protocols* forgery again in 1934 as folly and wickedness designed by corrupt minds. God would punish them. Stanley Frodsham labeled the *Protocols* as a mischievous attempt to whip up social hysteria against the Jewish people.[7]

When many of Hitler's Nazi atrocities against the Jewish people became known by the mid-1930s, the Assemblies of God called on Pentecostals to break with their isolationist past. It was time to defend the Jewish people. Pentecostals were warned that unless Nazism was stopped in Europe, American Jewish people could face the same nightmare.[8] Pentecostal Christians must never forget God's command: *"Pray for the peace of Jerusalem"* (Ps. 122:6).

The recounting of wartime atrocities by the Nazis against Jewish people horrified the 1943 *Pentecostal Evangel* readership. A dire warning followed against the possibility of American anti-Semitism in a land with ten times the Jewish people of Nazi Germany. America was far from free of prejudice against the Jewish people. Every Christian was duty bound to set his or her face against this danger.[9]

Satan had tried to destroy the Jewish people, Jesus' own people, on two counts, both spiritually and physically. Satan attacks the Jewish people because of their God-given destiny. Plainly, the Assemblies of God leadership wanted no part in any form of anti-Semitism.

JEWISH VIRTUE

The *Pentecostal Evangel* stated in 1931 that we owe everything we religiously enjoy to the Jewish people. The Church was born as a Messianic Jewish faith community. All later Christian persecution of the Jewish people was entirely without justification. God would soon establish the Jewish nation as "the head and not the tail" among the nations. The Jewish people were still the Chosen People with the fulfillment of marvelous God-given promises yet awaiting them.

The blame for Jewish resistance to the Gospel was laid at the feet of Christians in 1937. Because Christians had misrepresented the loving Jesus, His own extended Jewish family members associated Christian faith with Jewish pain. Jewish patriarchs and prophets had provided the richness of the biblical record for both Jewish and Christian benefit. Jewish people had been among the great American patriots. Jewish people like Haym Solomon, major financier of the American Revolution, had financially contributed significantly to each of the American wars. Jewish people had made significant contributions in medicine, music, astronomy, literature, and invention.

APPEAL TO PENTECOSTAL AMERICAN SELF-INTEREST

The *Pentecostal Evangel* made clear in 1933 that the Christian aspiration should always be to conform to God's nature. Since He loves and shows infinite mercy to the Jewish people, Christians should do the same. Jewish people had faced disgraceful persecution in much of Christendom. But in America, new light had dawned on Bible-based Christianity. It was now clear that we should honor Israel and cause them to rejoice. Henry Ford and other anti-Semites should be checked so that Jewish Americans would not be "wounded in the house of their friends."

The *Pentecostal Evangel* advocated that its readership should exhibit God's loving mercy toward Israel. But poor Christian attitude toward Jewish people earned renewed warning in 1934. Jewish people had been persecuted in all nations but America. That might be one reason God had so prospered America.[10]

Pentecostal Witness to the Jewish People

As one product of the Nazi propaganda machine, Pentecostal leadership confronted the common use of offensive language that insulted Jewish people. They cautioned Pentecostal youths in 1930 not to casually use words like "sheeny" even when without particularly evil intent. To do so was evil just the same. Such use of terms of reproach or contempt placed one in the awkward position of offending Christ Himself. The world despised the Jewish people.

Perhaps the Church mindlessly followed the world's lead in neglect and abuse of Jewish people.[11]

In 1943 the *Pentecostal Evangel* reported that Nazi hatred did not discriminate between the various social elements of the Jewish people. In his doctoral disseration, Mitch Glaser has shown that 250,000 of the Jewish people killed by the Nazis were Hebrew Christians.[12]

1945 General Council Resolution on Anti-Semitism

A resolution condemning anti-Semitism was adopted on the floor of the General Council of the Assemblies of God in the national bi-annual session in 1945. It recognized the alarming increase in anti-Semitism and declared itself opposed to it. Accepting the Scriptures as truth they recognized that God has redeemed Israel unto Himself to be His people forever. Despite Israel's failures, the Spirit of God tells us they are still "beloved for the fathers' sakes" (see Rom. 11:28). Like the apostle Paul, we are all called to be intercessors for Israel. If one prays for the people represented by Jerusalem, he will never be guilty of anti-Semitism.[13]

PENTECOSTAL IDEOLOGY ON ISRAEL'S DESTINY AND MESSIANIC FAITH

Between 1918 and 1945, Pentecostal ideology on Israel's ultimate destiny continued to develop and find greater clarity. They believed in the future of national Israel and her God-decreed destiny on biblical grounds. God would display to the universe His own intention for Israel as the last days unfolded. As Pentecostals shared their faith with the Jewish people, Israel should become that redeemed and faithful Messianic nation that God promised would affect global redemption. Only with this broad panorama of Pentecostal ideology can the historian and believer begin to fathom the essence of Zionism's romantic hold on the Pentecostal heart.

God's Purpose and Intention for Israel

Pentecostals remained persuaded that God had chosen to be with the indestructible Jewish people, the great miracle of history. The dawning of Israel's glorious new day was at hand. Israel would never again be nationally uprooted. Israel would reject the antichrist and turn to Jesus. At that point, an international confederation of armies would surround Israel, ready to devour them. The divine Deliverer and Messiah, Jesus, would then manifest from Heaven, take vengeance on Israel's enemies, and judge the nations. Then He would set up the glorious Davidic throne in Zion to reign over the nations from there for a thousand years.[14]

The fulfillment of Joel 2:23-32 would find its ultimate expression as the Holy Spirit richly anointed the Jewish people. Then the nations would benefit mightily as the finally restored nation of Israel walked in the multiplied blessings of God.

Though God had not yet fulfilled His purposes in Israel, the preservation of the Jewish people was a perpetual reality. Christians needed to understand the important role of Israel in God's program. Without the Jewish people there was no key to either Scripture or history. The world was in disorder and would remain so until Israel was divinely restored.[15]

Israel had been temporarily shelved but would be divinely reactivated when the Spirit's "full course of operation among the Gentiles" ended.[16] Gentiles had benefited by being grafted into "the good olive tree of spiritual blessings promised to Israel." But, as Romans 11 anticipated, Israel had only temporarily lost connection with the life flow and would soon be spiritually regrafted and their fullness restored.

Zionism—Prelude to Christ's Return

Pentecostals were ideologically committed to the ideal growth and development of the Zionist enterprise. They believed Zionism's success to be an immediate prelude to the summation of salvation history and the Second

Coming. As early as 1920, Pentecostals taught that Christians should pray for the restoration of the Jewish people to their land, for by this we may hasten the day of our Lord's coming. The Promised Land would have a geographical area at least ten times greater than that of Palestine and would blossom as the rose. Thousands of young Jewish people had arrived in Palestine, but Arab opposition had slowed the formation of a Jewish State. But as God promised, soon Jesus will come to reign at Jerusalem as King of kings and Lord of lords.

Pentecostals looked beyond the immediate problems in anticipation of Jerusalem as the center of the new nation, and Jewish people would formulate the development of the country. Much Pentecostal goodwill existed toward the Jewish people. God, by allowing current European political discomfort, was bringing Jewish people in large numbers back to Zion. Hitler's recent edict inspired 600,000 well-situated German Jewish people to look favorably on relocation to Zion to till the soil, and even contend with Arabs. But Christ alone could affect remedy for the struggling Jewish people. Jewish dependence on their own militia to deliver Jerusalem rather than dependence on God was considered vanity.[17]

Pentecostals seemed frustrated that at the present time neither the Jewish people nor Jesus were in their proper places. Reluctant Jewish people should quickly return to Zion in harmony with God's program. But Jewish people had demonstrated a propensity for following false messiahs. The Bible indicated that Israel would follow yet another false messiah, the antichrist. But Israel's call for divine deliverance would result in astounding new faith in Jesus. Startling tales of renewed Jewish interest and faith in Jesus inspired Pentecostal conviction that Jesus was coming soon.[18]

Ultimate Victory of the Israel of God

For Pentecostals, successful Zionistic land reclamation or a Jewish State in Zion would never suffice. Only Jewish restoration to God and renewal of the Kingdom covenant would do. Only then would Israel reenter the river of God's spiritual blessing and share that blessing with the world. Then anti-Semitism would be a thing of the past, and Jewish people would be highly esteemed. But Israel must fully repent. The keys to Israel's inheritance are repentance and faith. Pentecostals were encouraged to give copies of the Gospel of Matthew to American Jewish youth, confident that God's Word would yield spiritual prosperity for the Jewish people.[19]

Pentecostals observed the rising tide of anti-Semitism in the modern political arena. The coming Armageddon would make World War I "look like a flea bite. But, though unexpected by the nations, Jesus would come, fulfill his promise to Israel, and bring righteousness and peace to them."[20]

Fulfillment of Israel's Prophetic Mission

God had always planned to accomplish His purposes through the Jewish people. He issued types, teaching, covenant, and other provisions needed to make them His global witnesses. They would become a nation of Spirit-filled missionaries.[21] From the divine perspective, the prophecies were as good as completed.

Along with expecting Israel's spiritual redemption, Pentecostals were encouraged to favor the Jew. Saul of Tarsus and his Damascus Road experience were the archetype of Israel. In spite of living in a lawless, sin-sick world, true believers would soon see the dazzling brightness of the rise of the Sun of Righteousness. Heavenly outpourings of the Holy Spirit would save Israel and generate great revival among the Gentiles.[22] God's program for Israel had not changed in the least. He had not revoked His calling and giftings to Israel.

PENTECOSTAL FRATERNAL IDENTITY WITH ISRAEL

Pentecostals sensed a fraternal identification with the Jewish people on three bases from 1918–1945, according to their publications: (1) They were fellow restorationists; (2) They were team players in global Messianic redemption; and (3) They were dependent on the Spirit's infusion of life-energy for the success of their assigned divine mission.

The 1922 *Pentecostal Evangel* rejected a low view of the Church that expected Israel to overshadow it. Dispensationalism taught that the Church would decline as the restored kingdom approached. But Pentecostals expected the Church to be victorious. There would be corresponding spiritual elements in the Jewish world too. An orthodox Jewish community in Bochara (USSR) anticipated the coming of the Messiah as reported in the 1925 *Pentecostal Evangel*. Mysterious signs, heavenly messages, and the final portion of the Book of Daniel had convinced them.[23]

Pentecostals focused on Stalin's war on God and Christianity. It made life miserable for three million Jewish people living under Russian domination. The "Moscow Pharaoh" would not permit a grand departure of Israel, so Jewish people were slipping off to Palestine in smaller groups. But the 1931 *Latter Rain Evangel* advised that this current fulfillment of prophecy should thrill true Christians and make the indifferent know deepening shadows were gathering over the earth.[24]

A Gospel Publishing House teachers' manual cautioned that some erred by allegorizing biblical predictions for Israel so as to apply them to the Church. Such teachers mistakenly assigned all biblical blessings to the Church and left all the judgments for Israel. But God's promises for Israel will be literally fulfilled as Romans 9–11 showed.[25]

In 1935, the Assemblies of God adopted a significant repudiation of post-tribulation rapture—the idea that both Israel and the Church would remain on earth for the seven-year tribulation. Pentecostals, however, were not prepared, as were the traditional dispensationalists, to relegate the final proclamation of the Gospel to the tribulation or millennial Israel. Both Israel and the Church were God's people and were to work in harmony for God's purposes on earth.

E.S. Williams, in 1937, pointed out that blessing would be brought to the world by the restoration of the Jewish people. He added that for this reason we ought to be interested in the salvation of Jewish people.[26] Noel Perkins, head of the Department of Foreign Missions for the General Council of the

Assemblies of God, wrote, "If we are lovers of the Word of God, we shall be lovers of Israel." Stanley Frodsham called for prayer for the salvation of Israel, which will mean to the world, "life from the dead." Frodsham plainly saw Israel and Pentecostalism linked in the last days.[27]

ZIONISM AND PENTECOSTAL MISSION EFFORTS AMONG INTERNATIONAL ISRAEL

During this secondary period in American Pentecostalism, 1918–1945, Pentecostals continued to sense their profound relatedness to the Jewish people, the progeny of the patriarchs. Political involvement was not considered legitimate Christian activity. So they made calls for Pentecostal youth and others to share their Christian faith on several bases. First were the evidences of new Jewish openness to listening to the Gospel. Second, because of Jewish expectations of a coming Messiah, the time was ripe. Third, the presence of Jewish leaders in the Assemblies of God indicated high dividends for Jewish evangelism. It was a fruitful harvest season. Fourth, since a redeemed Israel would play such a crucial role in the last days leading to Christ's return, Jewish evangelism was consistent with God's end-time program. Pentecostal youth were encouraged to reflect the Spirit of Christ to Jewish people.

From 1920 on, there were many reports of thousands of Jewish people becoming Christians. The 1933 *Pentecostal Evangel* reported that many Jewish people were reluctant to embrace Christ out fear of alienation from Israel, but many were turning to Him with their eyes opened to Him as the God-given Savior and Messiah.[28] Jewish believer Andrew Marks testified in 1939 of Jewish responsiveness to the Gospel. Fifteen Jewish families and a rabbi who attended Assemblies of God evangelistic services in Illinois accepted Jesus. Pentecostals should pray for and evangelize Israel's lost sheep with loving-kindness.[29]

Another conviction undergirding Pentecostal evangelism among Jewish people was the tremendous fruitfulness this had yielded in recent times. In proportion to their numbers, Jewish believers entered Christian ministry three times more often than Gentile Christians. Significant was the unexpected testimony that most Jewish believers were brought to faith by Gentile Christians rather than by fellow Jewish people.[30]

To illustrate the value of sharing faith, the *Pentecostal Evangel* highlighted several outstanding Jewish Christian ministers. In 1924 it recounted the story of Joseph Wolf, a world-traveling Jewish ambassador for Christ.[31] He had important success even in the Islamic world. Another story was told of Michael Alexander, a rabbi who became an Anglican bishop in 1841 and later founded Christ Church within the Jaffa Gate of Jerusalem.[32]

Another impetus for Jewish evangelism was the conviction that it simply was the will of God. But preparation was needed to avoid needless offense. Armin Holzer printed in the *Latter Rain Evangel* his experiences as a new Christian and gave a host of examples of Christian anti-Semitism that negatively impacted Jewish understanding of Christianity.[33] Christian kindness was vitally needed as statistics proved nearly 98 percent of all Hebrew Christians first considered the Gospel after an act of Christian kindness. Ruth Angel, another Jewish believer, wrote to inform and inspire Pentecostal youth to engage in Jewish evangelism.[34]

The *Pentecostal Evangel* in 1929 told of persecution of the Jewish people and in 1932 urged Pentecostals to use the language of love when sharing the Gospel.[35] Pearlman, in 1935, said Pentecostal interest in Jewish people should be intense since God had such a glorious future for Israel.[36] Christians should not lose sight of the fact that Jesus was the legal King of Israel and belonged to the Jewish people. Jesus would yet lead Israel into a destiny in keeping with its calling to be a holy nation and kingdom of priests. When all Israel would embrace Christ, a new spiritual era for humankind would be opened.[37]

In 1942, Pearlman offered in the *Pentecostal Evangel* three guidelines as to what the Assemblies of God might do "to lead Israel from reproach to glory." First, the Church must take the right attitude toward the Jewish people. While Jewish people might not be superior to others individually, they had a national divinely assigned destiny distinct from others. Second, Christians could remind Jewish people that the first church was cradled in their nation. Third, Christians could appeal to Jewish people to identify themselves with Christ since He had so identified Himself with them.[38]

E.S. Williams, in 1944, called for greater efforts in Jewish evangelism in the light of Israel's present plight.[39] Ralph Riggs, later general superintendent of the Assemblies of God (1953–1959), in 1945 called for Jewish evangelism out of regard for Jesus' love for His own Jewish people.[40]

PENTECOSTAL MISSIONS IN THE LAND OF ISRAEL

Early missionary Florence Bush testified to Jerusalem's Jewish people of Jesus and the Second Coming. She termed Jerusalem a dark place, but wrote in 1914 of seven or eight young Jewish people who stood to profess confidence of their personal salvation in Jesus.[41]

Jewish people of Jerusalem reportedly rose at 3:30 every morning to cry and mourn in prayer as they recited psalms on the cold stone floor. Immigrants from Russia were arriving in an attempt to perpetuate traditional Judaism. They believed Judaism would be lost in Russia after the 1917 revolution. Jewish missionary Elizabeth Brown petitioned Weekly Evangel readers in 1918 to offer prayer and material support for the needs of Jerusalem. She also reported hardships in Jerusalem including food and housing shortages. The Jewish bitterness she encountered in Jerusalem was worse than she had seen in previous evangelistic efforts in Chicago, New York, and Pittsburgh.[42]

Sara Radford, new Assemblies of God missionary to Jerusalem, noted in the 1924 Pentecostal Evangel that mourners at the Wailing Wall were filled with conviction of the soon restoration of Israel's national glory. But they were not turning to Jesus. The need for spiritual refreshing made the missionaries long for a new outpouring of the Latter Rain.

Another new missionary, Vida Baer, was expecting great change. The Assemblies of God rented facilities in Jerusalem in 1924 for congregational meetings. Baer asked for prayer for special evangelistic meetings. Zionists came into the mission to listen by night with a tear, a sob, and a "Why?".

But by 1925 large numbers of Jerusalem's Jewish people had confessed faith, been river-baptized, and were ready to read the Hebrew New Testament. As his own way of expediting the Second Coming, one elderly Jewish believer in Jerusalem bought all the Bibles he could locate to place in hotels. In the same year, the *Pentecostal Evangel* reported that a Messianic congregation of 70 Jewish people had formed in Tiberias.[43]

Walter Fuchs, newly appointed Assemblies of God missionary to Tel Aviv, found a group of nominal Christian Jewish people hungry for the full Gospel. In 1928, he told of a Jewish veterinary surgeon healed of eczema. He had several extremely positive encounters with Jewish people, but he had to keep relocating in order to avoid terrible persecution by fellow Jewish people against new Jewish believers.[44] In 1931, however, Beskin reported that Jewish people were demonstrating more acceptance and allowing Jewish believers rights to their opinion.[45] Then in 1935 Vera Swarzrauber described rapidly improving life for Jewish people. The Spirit of God was again moving.[46] The answer to Jewish resistance to the Gospel was an even stronger dose of Pentecostalism.

INTERNATIONAL JEWISH RESPONSE
TO JESUS, 1918–1945

Over time, Pentecostal awareness of Jewish responsiveness to the Gospel extended to include Jewish mission activities worldwide. The *Pentecostal Evangel* reported increased Jewish response to Christ in 1924. The times of the Gentiles ran out along with the lifting of Israel's blindness when Jerusalem was wrested from Turkish hands in 1917. The Spirit of God was moving. Also Ukrainian Jewish people had developed interest in Christ. They had formed

Hebrew Christian assemblies that retained their independence by refusing support from denominations.[47]

Two Jewish spiritual transformations were accented in 1924: those of Hans Herzl, son of Theodor Herzl, and Joseph Rabinowitz, colonizing scout sent to Palestine by the Jewish people in Kishineff, Russia. Herzl was baptized in the Baptist church in Vienna. Rabinowitz came to faith while reading the Hebrew New Testament on the Mount of Olives. He returned to Russia telling his synagogue audience that the key to the Holy Land was Jesus.[48]

Enthusiastic reports in 1925 told of Jewish missionary work in Tunisia and Ethiopia. Groups of Polish Jewish people of 500–1,200 packed meeting rooms and churches to hear the Gospel. Philip Lewis, a London Jew, had won 6,000 Australians to Christ. Thousands more European Jewish people had joined Christian churches. Some 40,000 Jewish people had become Christians in Hungary since 1918. Pearlman noted in 1929 that about 600 Jewish people were preaching the Gospel throughout Europe. This was significant in light of the persecution Jewish believers endured including bitter hatred, loss of employment, banishment from beloved Jewish communities, and loss of family and friends. Yet many still came, including Alexander Kaminsky, the last Czar's court violinist and concertmaster of the Imperial Grand Opera orchestra. He surrendered his profession and enormous income to use his talents for the Lord he loved.[49]

AMERICAN ASSEMBLIES OF GOD JEWISH MISSIONS

As always, good news from Zion brought enthusiasm for the prospect of improved missionary opportunities. But Pentecostals could not ignore the millions of American Jewish people. Charles Spellman, missionary in Los Angeles, appealed for more Jewish evangelistic involvement in the 1921 *Pentecostal Evangel*. He expressed his grief for millions of American Jewish people who were drifting into atheism and materialism. He believed that Jewish people had their greatest opportunity to witness the purest form of Christianity in America.[50]

John Mark Levy's book, Christianity the Flower and Fruit of Judaism, was highly touted in the 1923 *Pentecostal Evangel*. He made a strong New Testament case that new Jewish believers were spiritually free to observe Israel's national rites and ceremonies.

The 1928, *Pentecostal Evangel* told of Constantin Brunner, son of a rabbi, who called for Jewish people to examine Jesus' "profound and holy words." He said they must be heard in the synagogues and taught to Jewish children for good and blessing, so that Jesus may find those He had been seeking. But in 1931 the *Latter Rain Evangel* reported a protest in an Orthodox Jewish newspaper against Jewish university students in Austria and Hungary who were studying the New Testament, praying to Jesus, shouting, and getting blessed.[51]

Jewish rabbis had also come to faith, according to Norman Beskin. In San Francisco a rabbi and many of his congregation were baptized and formed the Jewish Christian Baptist Church. Beskin also reported that 300,000 Jewish people had turned to Christ across America in recent years. Jewish study groups to investigate the New Testament were established in cities like Wichita, Kansas.[52] It seemed that dramatic persecution of Jewish believers was a thing of the past.

Assemblies of God confidence in the future redemption of Israel inspired support for yet more evangelistic efforts among the Jewish people. Meyer Tan Ditter, one of their appointed missionaries in Chicago, insisted that there had always been a remnant of Jewish Christians down through the ages. There were still many in 1938. Many more would believe if some would hear the call and take the message of Christ to the Jewish people.[53]

Alexander Marks, another of their Jewish missionaries in Chicago, commended Pentecostal evangelism of the Jewish people. They were multilingual, and their ability to acclimate themselves to new regions would predispose them to be good missionaries. The Pentecostal approach would capture their hearts and minds of the five million American Jewish people who needed the message.[54] The next year, the Home Missions department sought resources to evangelize the 400,000 Jewish residents and refuges in the Chicago area.

THE UNIQUE CORRELATION BETWEEN GLOSSOLALIA AND THE JEWISH PEOPLE

There were no Gentiles among the 3,000 saved on the Day of Pentecost. Later, Gentile Christian leaders led the Church away from its Jewish roots and Pentecostal practices. But the unique experience of tongue-speaking in the 20th century benefited the Gentile church and assisted in the restoration of Jewish people. Thus, Jewish Pentecostal experience affirmed Pentecostal restorationism and gave it significant support.

D.W. Kerr (1856–1927), pastor and educator, reported in the 1921 *Latter Rain Evangel* that an unbelieving Jew came into a San Jose healing meeting. Dramatic healings convinced him that Jesus is the living Messiah. He said that now he saw that salvation in Jesus had been his Jewish inheritance all along, but that he had never before recognized Christ.[55]

Stanley Frodsham, in 1926, recounted a series of Pentecostal episodes involving Jewish people. One example was Lewis Rudner, a 26-year-old Austrian Jew, who had spoken Hebrew from childhood. In Seattle, he saw a welcome sign on a mission building, went in, and heard a man reciting Isaiah 53 in Hebrew, a woman singing a Rosh HaShanah hymn, and a 12-year-old girl reciting Psalms 12 and 6 in Hebrew. A black woman began repeating Jeremiah 33 in Hebrew. Then a Scandinavian woman pointed to Rudner and in Hebrew explained his lost condition and need to turn to God. Soon they all gathered around him earnestly praying in Hebrew. When Rudner realized he was not in a synagogue and the people had no Hebrew background, he began to cry out to God in Hebrew for mercy and became a Christian.[56]

Dr. Frances Murcutt happened into a Pentecostal meeting in Portland when a man began speaking to her in purest Parisian French, a language she knew. This man, who knew not a word of French, perfectly explained the way of salvation, told her of the Latter Rain and urged her to yield to God. Murcutt fell on her knees, yielded to God, and became a beloved Assemblies of God personality.[57]

Maurice Kullman, a Jew and a Baptist pastor, was outraged when his wife became a Pentecostal. One night she began to pray in Hebrew, perfectly articulating even the guttural sounds. This convinced him of the supernatural nature of the Pentecostal experience, and he received Spirit-baptism and spoke in tongues.[58]

Zelma Argue told of an 8-year-old Jewess in Chicago who came to a meeting for healing. After lying under the power of the Spirit for hours, she asked to be lifted to a chair. She then recounted her highly descriptive vision of war and concluded with a series of woes. World War I began the next year.[59]

Frodsham heard a fellow Pentecostal speak in Hebrew. A rabbinical student was present and took the Hebrew message as a sign from God. That evening he received a vision of Calvary, the resurrection, ascension, and Second Coming. Many recognized this as a fulfillment of Isaiah 28:11-13 before their eyes. Frodsham called for prayer that God, who had given signs and wonders at Israel's beginning, would give Israel signs and wonders again.[60]

A 1942 column of the *Pentecostal Evangel* labeled "Witnessing to Jews: Speaking Languages They Understand," printed a letter from Alma Crosby of Beaumont, Texas. She told of Pentecostal encounters with Jewish people. One was a frustrated secretary who went with her to an Assemblies of God congregation. Crosby prayed with her, and she was baptized in the Holy Spirit. She left the young Jewess lying prostrate with Christ's glory radiating from her face as she spoke in a heavenly language.[61]

Another time, a hospitalized old Jewess was nearly dead from diabetes. Doctors intended to amputate her leg. She asked Crosby for prayer. Mrs. Crosby suddenly began speaking in tongues in a peculiar language. The startled Jewess identified it as Rumanian and gave the interpretation, urging her to get forgiveness of sins. She immediately raised her hands and accepted Jesus. Then she regularly attended the Assemblies of God congregation giving constant testimony about the wonders of Jesus.[62]

Clearly, the Jewish people desperately needed the Pentecostal gospel. By it they would obtain a place of spiritual usefulness to God. Signs, wonders, and miracles would be vital to speedily bring Israel to faith and reconciliation to God.

Chapter 5

PENTECOSTALISM'S IDEOLOGY OF MESSIANIC ZIONISM (1946–1972)

During the Great Depression and German Nazism's rise to power in the 1930s, American Pentecostalism witnessed a decline in religious fervor. It became increasingly apparent that the pristine 1st-century apostolic Christianity the founders envisioned had generally evaded them. The delay of the grand impetus for Pentecostalism, the Second Coming, caused a new generation to question Latter Rain eschatological assumptions regarding both the full restoration of the Church and the imminence of Zion's biblical destiny.

Many Pentecostals were ready to discard their long-term "rejected" label and move into the social embrace of respectable Christian society. Evangelicals appealed to them to join the National Association of Evangelicals to make prophetic protest against the loss of Christian values. This afforded Pentecostals a platform to speak to American society in a manner superior to anything previously imagined possible.

Pentecostal leadership recognized changes would have to be made if they were to be socially acceptable to their new Evangelical friends. Older cultural taboos and anti-intellectualism would have to be constrained. Significantly too, the conviction of fraternal-twin apostolic restoration alongside a Zionist-inspired national Israel would also require some accommodations. Some found clear Pentecostal identification with the most persecuted people in the world to be increasingly distasteful. Worse, the revival of national Israel in 1948 did not guarantee Israel's political survival as enemies threatened them. How might Pentecostal credibility fare if the new Jewish State went up in Muslim ashes? Pragmatism called for placing some distance between Pentecostalism's self-legitimization and its enthusiasm for a restored Israel.

From the end of World War II and into the 1950s, there was a gradual lessening of unswerving Pentecostal support for the Jewish state. Some cautioned against overdue confidence in the Jewish nation prior to Israel's messianic faith in Jesus. Some even denied divine involvement in Zionist aspirations. By 1961, the Assemblies of God actually changed its Statement of Fundamental Truths to push the eschatological salvation of national Israel into the millennium, as dispensationalists held.

The newer Latter Rain, healing, and charismatic movements in the late 1940s, 1950s, and 1960s might ignore Israel without particular consequence to their self-understanding. But the Assemblies of God had no such luxury. Its restoration theology was identified fraternally with Zion's hope of restoration. So it could not ignore the issue of the modern state of Israel. Therefore, many Assemblies of God theologians had to devote much scholastic energy to the Zionist role in the endtimes.

Soon after the State of Israel was established in 1948, the Assemblies of God retreated from its unqualified support of Zionism. Their hope for Israel centered on Jewish national faith in Jesus. So they turned to intensified evangelistic efforts in Israel and among Jewish people in the United States. But there was an anticlimax to three generations of Jewish mission efforts in Israel. The Assemblies of God sold its only piece of prime property in the heart of Jerusalem to the Greek Orthodox in 1969, just two years after Israel's recapture of Jerusalem in the 1967 Six Day War. It was then resold to Conservative Judaism who continue to maintain religious services there at the bustling intersection of Agron, Keren HaYesod, and King George Streets.

SOCIAL IMPACT UPON AMERICAN PENTECOSTALISM (1946–1972)

Pentecostal Upward Mobility

Societal change after World War II had a dramatic effect on Pentecostal identity and social practice. New levels of American political influence and international trade promised new prosperity. This progressively enticed Pentecostals into a mostly new role as members of America's middle class. Increased wealth led to new pursuit of educational opportunities. No longer was higher education perceived as the death knell to spirituality. The gap continually widened between earlier ideals perceived as biblical and the new reality of prosperity.[1]

More Pentecostal children were sent to college. The string of Assemblies of God Bible Institutes first established across America in the 1920s and 1930s became full colleges and pursued full accreditation by the 1960s. Evangel College (now Evangel University) became the first Assemblies of God liberal arts college in 1955. The Assemblies of God Graduate School (now the Assemblies of God Theological Seminary) was established by 1972. The academic training, not only of clergy but also of teachers, nurses, businesspeople, mathematicians, and scientists of many varieties, reflected the movement's desire for integration into the larger American milieu. The emphasis on academic scholarship also helped eliminate some of the social stigma of anti-intellectualism.

Middle Class Values

From the early 1960s, the Assemblies of God mirrored the same cultural bewilderment of most denominations. American culture was in social foment and general disarray. American youth were increasingly alienated from traditional churches. Americans became fixated on a moral pluralism with the breakdown of core American values. The pursuit of the almighty dollar evoked a strong reaction from university-age youth. Tens of thousands of highly pro-filed, drug-using, free-loving hippies protested against moral structures. In fatalistic despair of societal survival, an increasing number of Americans used drugs and engaged in promiscuous sexual practices. In this cultural morass, the Assemblies of God began mobilizing for massive evangelism.[2]

During the 1960s and early 1970s, Assemblies of God membership grew. Christians of other denominations, such as Presbyterian, Methodist, and Episcopal, were drawn to the more vivacious and increasingly middle-class Congregations. However, this led to erosion of commitment to the denomination and to specific Pentecostal tenets. Soon Pentecostals began to be preoccupied with numbers. American success ideals that believe bigger is better replaced many valued signs of Pentecostal humility. Too often chasing the American dream of material abundance proved to be a hazard to traditional Pentecostal identity. Material success and social position became the marks of status rather than genuine Pentecostal spirituality.

The Allure of the National Association of Evangelicals

During their first four decades, both Fundamentalist and Holiness denominations denounced Pentecostals, while the balance of Western Christianity largely ignored them. This began to change when Evangelical, Holiness, and Fundamentalist groups invited Pentecostals to enlist in the 1942 creation of the National Association of Evangelicals (NAE). Most of the hundreds of smaller Pentecostal groups refused, seeing this as a step toward worldliness. But the Assemblies of God was quite ready to make whatever accommodation necessary to find acceptance among these non-Pentecostals.[3]

The National Association of Evangelicals intended from the outset to establish a highly visible platform to corporately accomplish what they could never do as single denominations. They hoped to advocate and promote conservative Christian causes in the American religious and political arenas. They would be up front to represent conservative congregations before government agencies and would demonstrate corporate Christian resolve to oppose the promotion of infidelity and apostasy.

Pentecostal entry into the National Association of Evangelicals brought sectarian opposition from many fundamentalist groups. For example, fundamentalist leader, Carl McIntire, assailed Pentecostals in his periodical, *Christian Beacon*, denouncing tongues as a great sign of apostasy. But the National Association of Evangelicals refused to join with him and chose to reach out to Pentecostals. They were in the minority in the Association in the 1940s and 1950s but soon moved into the majority.[4]

After their long experience of rejection, the Assemblies of God leadership happily identified with the newer Evangelicalism. They began to classify themselves as "Evangelicals plus" or as evangelicals energized by a spiritual experience. From this platform, they could lay claim to the richness of evangelical history and envision a glorious future. In spite of some protests, they became full partners with Evangelicals seeking to regain paradise lost, that is, the former Christian America. The rise of the Charismatic movement in the classical Protestant churches in the late 1950s and 1960s helped to overcome the cultural breach between "disinherited" Pentecostals and the major denominations.

Along with this was a gradual relaxation of emphasis on the Second Coming. Though Pentecostals would continue to proclaim Christ's coming for decades to come, tongues speaking became the central tenet of Pentecostalism. As tongues speaking became more linked to the weekly worship experience, the diminished emphasis on eschatology suggested decreasing relevance of immediate events on the Zionist front. This explains how the Pentecostal romance with Israel could more easily ebb and flow during the mid-century than in the more resolute years of early Pentecostalism.

MODIFICATION OF PENTECOSTALISM'S IMAGE

Dismantling of the Rejectionist Front

Abandonment of Pentecostalism's radical origins significantly contributed to their numerical growth. Tongue speakers from all backgrounds and religious persuasions were embraced by mid-century. However, the Assemblies of God, along with Evangelicals, were still reluctant to trust or welcome unity with mainstream Protestant or Catholic Christianity. Even so, more conservative members of the National Association of Evangelicals kept Pentecostals distant. This further motivated the Assemblies of God to make more concessions to appease Evangelicals by modifying classical Pentecostal restorationism.

Rejection of the "New Order of the Latter Rain" (1948–1949)

Theological squabblings, political machinations, and the utter humanity of Pentecostals helped cool the fever-pitched expectation for pristine apostolic restoration. For many it became apparent that due to human frailties, true Church apostolic restoration might only follow Christ's return. Therefore, Pentecostals like Frank Boyd and E.S. Williams increasingly used dispensationalism to affirm that the Church would largely apostatize and the world would sink into chaos in the endtimes. The delay of the Second Coming clarified there would be a longer-term involvement in the present dispensation than originally anticipated.

As local Pentecostal worship services lost much of their ecstatic expression, a longing for earlier days grew. One hopeful answer came out of the 1947 Pentecostal revival in a remote Bible school in North Battleford, Saskatchewan, Canada. It soon spread and was quickly dubbed the "New Order of the Latter Rain." It obviously reached back to the Latter Rain emphasis in earlier Pentecostalism. It sought the same zeal for the miraculous, was excited about the Second Coming, and repudiated organized religion.[5] But it soon developed extreme positions. Especially chosen "New Order" apostles and prophets began to function with rigid authority. It claimed every generation is to experience its own pristine restoration of New Testament apostolic Christianity.

The twenty-third General Council of the Assemblies of God in 1949 took official action to disapprove the "New Order of the Latter Rain" for many reasons. They had overemphasized the imparting of spiritual gifts by the laying on of hands and prophecy. They had taught that the Church is built on the foundation of present-day apostles and prophets. In deliverance ministry, they had claimed prerogatives to human agency that belong only to Christ. They had claimed to impart gifts of languages for missionary service. They had told young people whom to marry and gave personal leadings to others by tongues and prophecy.

A most astounding realization is the apparent total disconnection of the New Order of the Latter Rain from Zionism even in 1948. They focused entirely on the restoration of apostolic Christianity without regard to Jewish people, Judaism, Zion, or Israel. This detachment from all things Jewish would equally characterize much of the later healing and deliverance revivalism of the 1950s, the Charismatic movement of the 1960s, and the Jesus movement that erupted on the heels of the Six Day War in 1967. Part of the reason for this was that none of them felt any need to embrace dispensationalism. They tended to regard modern Israel as a political development fashioned by human efforts alone.

MOVEMENT AWAY FROM RESTORATIONIST IDEOLOGY AND ISRAEL

By 1961, the Assemblies of God had made a series of adjustments to alter its image before a watching Christian America. It assuaged its traditional codes of conduct thereby orchestrating a new commonality with many who shared the pursuit of an Evangelical redemption of American culture. Its leaders grew increasingly aloof from its earlier firm commitments to Zionism. However, grassroots pastors and laymen still highly favored Zion and firmly supported American foreign policy on Israel.[6]

The faith-healing movement of the 1950s created new tensions in the Assemblies of God. So did Charismatic ecumenical efforts by men like David DuPlessis. They revealed the readiness of grassroots enthusiasts to reach back to many of the radical Latter Rain foundations as they pursued spiritual power and unity. The Pentecostal Golden Age was not past to these Spirit-baptized enthusiasts—but both present and future. Yet their efforts to restore 1st-century Pentecostalism had two chief surprises for classical restorationists. First, Christians pouring in from historic churches had not been conditioned to think in eschatological terms. They did not necessarily attach divine significance to the rise of Israel. Second, Israel bore no particular relevance to their interaction with the Spirit.

Easing eschatological tensions related to the Second Coming dramatically lessened the immediate significance of Zionism or the State of Israel. Both were dispensationally pushed off into the millennium. A significant and subtle change came with the 1961 modification of Article 14 of the Assemblies of God Statement of Fundamental Truths. In 1927, it read,

> The revelation of the Lord Jesus Christ from *heaven*, the *salvation of national Israel* and the millennial reign of Christ on earth are the Scriptural promises and the world's hope (2 Thess. 1:7; Rev. 19:11-14; Rom. 11:26-27; Rev. 20:1-7,15). (My emphasis.)

This was changed to be brought into greater conformity with the National Association of Evangelicals propositions. The new 1961 reading was:

> The second coming of Christ includes the rapture of the saints, which is our blessed hope, followed by visible return of Christ with His saints to reign on earth for one thousand years (Zech. 14:5; Matt. 24:27, 30; Rev. 1:7; 19:11-14;

20:1-6). *This millennium will bring the salvation of national Israel* (Ezek. 37:21-22; Zeph. 3:19-20; Rom. 11:26-27) and the establishment of universal peace (Ps. 73:3-8; Isa. 11:6-9; Mic. 4:3-4). (My emphasis.)

This second version was a more careful embrace of classical premillennial dispensationalism. It clearly put off the fraternal-twin restorationist fulfillment to the millennial future. Israel was now expected to remain temporarily in unbelief. By it, Pentecostals submitted to the dispensational tenet of a basically defeated Church that would be raptured out of the fray rather than be restored.

This decrease of the romantic Zionist expectation caused Pentecostals to emphasize that Israel's grand destiny would be held in abeyance pending Israel's full repentance and national embrace of Jesus. They also offered disclaimers against indiscriminate endorsement of Israeli policies. They did not want to damage the Assemblies of God image in the Islamic world, since they saw its great need of missionary activity.

THE SHIFTING ROMANCE OF ZION AND THE STATE OF ISRAEL (1946–1972)

The romantic Pentecostal fascination with Zionism and the restoration of the State of Israel continued into the 1970s. Growing Jewish population figures, land reclamation projects, new cities, new colleges, religious and business news, and overcoming of threats all held much of Assemblies of God readership spellbound. In spite of lessening dependence upon Zionism for ideological support, more than 50 percent of the weekly issues of the *Pentecostal Evangel* in 1950 contained multiple articles or news clips on modern Israel. There can be no doubt of continued Pentecostal affections for Zion and the State of Israel on the popular grassroots level.

The five chief scholastic influences upon the Assemblies of God between 1946 and 1972 were Myer Pearlman, Frank M. Boyd, Ralph M. Riggs, Ernest

S. Williams, and Stanley M. Horton. Each had very strong sentiments toward Zionism and the restoration of the State of Israel. With the exception of Stanley Horton, they all favored a general embrace of dispensationalism. All were recognized educators and prolific writers. Their texts were used in Bible institutes and colleges, in Pentecostal pulpits, and in local church educational programs across America. Meanwhile, the popular writings of C.M. Ward, Louis Hauff, and Gordon Lindsay helped maintain Pentecostal expectation for providential activity in Zion at the grassroots level.

Following his premature death in 1943, Myer Pearlman's influence lingered into the 1950s and 1960s, since his titles continued to be used in Bible institutes and colleges.[7] Pearlman clearly advocated that Israel's restoration was not a distant eschatological event but a reality on the immediate horizon. While generally holding to dispensationalism, for Pearlman, Israel and the Church were in real continuity. He saw the Church as an expansion and extension of the spiritually regenerated remnant of Israel. All Israel will be saved and, with the Church, will be part of the Bride of Christ.[8]

In 1945, Ralph M. Riggs wrote *The Bible's Backbone*, which became an important influence on the Assemblies of God for decades. He was confident that prior to the kingdom of Israel's Messianic establishment, Jewish people would undergo a severe season of chastening (the time of Jacob's trouble), due to rejection of the Gospel.[9] But the millennium would see a mighty outpouring the Spirit on the Jewish people.[10]

The fuller revelation of Nazi atrocities and the Jewish people caused the Assemblies of God to sense a responsibility to address the horrors of anti-Semitism. The 1945 General Council passed a resolution condemning it. Pentecostal literature promoted goodwill toward Jewish people and pointed out the immense price past anti-Semitic nations had paid.

By November 1948, the Gospel Publishing House taught that few coming events in Scripture are as identifiable as the restoration of the Jewish people. The progeny of the ancient Israelites were going back home, waste places were being rebuilt, the land was being tilled, and the United States had recognized the new nation.

The 1948 *Pentecostal Evangel* noted that while the Zionists accepted the United Nations offer of two states, the Arab league declared a jihad upon the United Nations. Consistent with God's intention for Israel, He would bring judgment on Muslim nations. Arab refusal to read the Scriptures would not change God's reality. He had not cast away His people Israel. The 20th-century outpouring of the Spirit was still linked to the Jewish return in this publication.[11]

Stanley Frodsham, in 1948, wrote of the utter vanity of international and historical efforts to destroy the Jewish people. The Muslims should recognize that, according to the Bible, to be an enemy of Israel was to be an enemy of God.[12]

The 1948 *Pentecostal Evangel* repudiated any lingering Christian notion that the Church had eternally replaced Israel in God's program. Rather, Israel's dry bones were being reassembled and would ultimately nationally live infused by God's own breath.[13] Frank M. Boyd wrote in his Introduction to Prophecy that the teaching of replacement of Israel by the Church was the result of misguided biblical interpretation that wrongly applied promises of Israel's restoration to the Church as spiritual Israel. Israel will experience its own Pentecostal outpouring in the millennium, and the Shechinah glory will overshadow Jerusalem.[14]

The rebirth of Israel was heralded as a divine miracle in 1948. After six months of intensive warfare, the little Jewish State not only warded off the attacks of 24 million Muslims but actually gained territory. Biblical prophecy was beginning to be fulfilled. The promises of the land were as reliable as all other biblical testimony.

In answer to criticism of Israel, the *Pentecostal Evangel* clarified that Jewish people purchased land from Arabs at exorbitant prices. A new exodus of Jewish people from Europe had benefited Arabs financially, educationally, and scientifically. But no earthly harmony could exist while the divine program was discounted. Therefore, Pentecostals needed to be aggressive both in their prayers and their evangelistic efforts to bring speedy spiritual redemption to Israel.[15]

Earnest S. Williams, in 1950, expected that now that Jerusalem was the capital of Israel, the restoration of the sacrificial system and the Second Coming were near at hand. But as long as Israel's King Jesus was rejected, Jerusalem would be trodden down by the Gentiles.[16] Since 1918, Pentecostal literature had indicated that Allenby's retaking of Jerusalem had been the point at which Jerusalem was no longer trodden down by the Gentiles. But 1948 forced the moving of the prophetic marker. Jerusalem was still trodden down as long as Arabs governed Jerusalem. What had been accomplished to date was but a foretaste of what was on the prophetic horizon.

The 1950 *Pentecostal Evangel* saw hopeful signs for the spiritual transformation of Israel. For example, Chaim Weizmann, British chemist and the first Israeli president, invited two rabbis to function as court prophets to religiously criticize government policies as needed.[17] Rabbi Henry Berkowitz said publicly that Jesus was "the very flowering of Judaism" and the "gentlest and noblest Rabbi of them all." Albert Einstein declared he was "enthralled by the luminous figure of the Nazarene."[18] Rabbi Stephen Wise protested against Jewish ignorance of the meaning of Christ.[19] Significant numbers of Israelis were clamoring for complete Christian Bibles in Hebrew.[20]

Nevertheless, by 1951, as the Arab world threatened to drive the Israelis into the sea, the *Pentecostal Evangel* felt compelled to address those who protested that Jewish terrorists had seized political control. Such activities could not be God's doing. The Jewish people needed Jesus. What had happened was perhaps not the final restoration, but it had certainly set the stage for the climax of the age. Both restorationist and dispensationalist camps agreed that an unbelieving Israel could not fully inherit the patriarchal blessings or find security in a Messianic era apart from national faith in Jesus. Restorationists sensed a missionary obligation to encourage Israel's spiritual awakening and active faith in Jesus. But dispensationalists, despairing of Israel's national salvation in the present age, were only prepared to accept Jewish people one by one into the Church.

As Arab threats lingered, the *Pentecostal Evangel* put out a still stronger disclaimer in 1952 against placing too much stock in current events in the unrepentant Jewish State of Israel. Jerusalem was still trodden down of the Gentiles. The current partial regathering was not the prophesied ultimate Messianic ingathering. God would not be satisfied with mere physical and material restoration. God's great purpose was to restore Israel to Himself and circumcise their hearts to love Him.

Boyd offered in the 1952 *Pentecostal Evangel* that only the Great Tribulation would finally bring Israel to national repentance and the embrace of Jesus as Messiah.[21] He had advocated for four decades that an era of grief and pain even greater than the Holocaust was on the Jewish horizon, since only greater suffering would affect Israel's national faith in Christ.

The theme denying modern Israel's identification with eschatological Israel continued in the 1953 *Pentecostal Evangel*. It would be wrong to confuse the amazing accomplishment of the present State of Israel with the glorious destiny of the nation promised in the Bible.[22] The return of Israel to Zion had been motivated by anything but spiritual causes. Israel was materialistic and largely atheistic. With all that stated, the Second Coming was still considered near. God allowed Israel's return to Zion to set the stage for Christ's return. A panicked Israel would finally cry out in desperation against the antichrist to receive God's answer to Israel's need: the Messiah Jesus.

With direct implications for Zionism, Ernest S. Williams taught that spiritual gifts were enablements for building up the Church and only secondarily given as signs for the confirmation of gospel truth to the world. He wanted people to think of tongues speaking as primarily for private use in prayer and public worship. Those filled could be expected to overflow to the benefit of others. Perhaps unwittingly, Williams was reducing the eschatological connection between Pentecostalism and Zionism.[23]

Riggs offered counter-balance to Williams when he stressed that the purpose for Spirit-baptism is primarily enduement with power for gospel witnessing. He saw Jewish national restoration even in a divided land as proving we are in the last days. By reaching back to restorationist beginnings, he was demonstrating the ongoing struggle with ambiguity Pentecostals would face in transitioning from restorationism to Pentecostal dispensationalism.[24]

Stanley Horton (b. 1916) was the rare multi-graduate-degreed academic Pentecostal in the 1950s when Pentecostals were still highly suspicious of secular university or graduate education.[25] But Horton's *Into All Truth*, published in 1955, is significant to our observation of the "shifting romance" of the Assemblies of God with Zionism and the State of Israel. Horton rejected dispensationalism while retaining a premillennial Second Coming teaching. This is significant inasmuch as it departed from the general Assemblies of God academic trend toward dispensationalism—a trend that ignored dispensationalism's inherent rejection of Pentecostalism, its low ecclesiology, and its placing providential accomplishment in Zion off into the utopian future. Horton moved away from a bleak destiny for Israel centering on severe judgments and more Jewish pain. He did recognize divine chastening possibly could be required to bring Israel to a place of necessary genuine repentance. Yet, the real change for Israel would come with an encounter with the Holy Spirit in characteristic Pentecostal fashion. Horton's text made clear the affinity between Pentecostalism and Israel's rebirth. There would be no climactic spiritual experience for Israel apart from the Spirit of God. In this view, the Pentecostal role corresponds to that of the Hebrew prophets. Pentecostal prophets could function in the spirit of Elijah and prepare the nation of Israel to receive God's best.

Horton wrote, "Through the Spirit would come the future blessings of Israel and the fulfillment of God's plan for them." Through God's prophets the "activity of the Spirit-directed men...made it possible for God to rid Israel of idolatry and prepare the way for Christ."[26] The Spirit of God alone can change Israel and transform the Jewish people into the people God truly wanted them to be. The Spirit and Word of God would then "find a real and permanent place in God's People." God's promise to Israel of a new covenant will bring Israel home, provide Israel with a new heart and spirit, and make the people of Israel the dwelling place of God's Spirit. Israel's return to Zion was but "the first step toward putting His Spirit in them."[27]

Israel continued to enjoy that "special place in God's plan" as Israel would yet pass the promised blessing on to a world in need. God's plan for humankind "is always related to God's dealings with Israel."[28]

Horton's ideology of Israel more closely resembled that of early restorationism. He did not require another time of severe Jewish persecution or chastening comparable to the Holocaust. Rather, the purging ministry of the Holy Spirit is sufficient to fully purify Israel. She would have a glowing Pentecostal encounter with the sanctifying Spirit of God.

One of the most outstanding voices in the mid-century Pentecostal movement was that of Revivaltime radio broadcaster Charles Morse Ward. His immense popularity and prolific writings impacted American understanding of Israel and the Jewish people. In 1955, he defended Israel against increasing criticism that they had caused the Palestinian refugee problem. He pointed out that Israel did not compel Palestinian Arabs to leave their homes. In fact, Israel besought Arabs to remain and help rebuild the land. They would enjoy every benefit of continuing in their homes and livelihoods. However, nothing Israel did could induce the Arabs to stay. The Arabs became refugees because they succumbed to Arab propaganda.[29]

Ward expressed his profound affection for the Jewish people by indicating that they were built on monotheism and had provided the very "breath of western civilization." Palestine was the cradle of every godly blessing. Rome contributed much to Western law and order and Athens to Western culture. But it "was Israel that provided 'soul'...the conscience and heart-beat of this world."[30]

Ward made it clear that freedom of religion, as understood by Americans, was virtually impossible in Islamic states. Islam considered conversion to anything non-Islamic an act of treason. However, God would have the last word. God had chosen Israel to be "a repository of redemptive truth" and would again make Israel "a great missionary nation."[31]

In 1956, Israel joined a French and British coalition against Nasser's Egyptian nationalization of the Suez Canal. In the heat of controversy Ward wrote that the "Jewish race will never be annihilated—never!"[32] Jewish history baffles unbelievers and the enemies of God.

Ward accepted the idea of the outpouring of wrath on Israel during the Great Tribulation. But he distinguished it as satan's wrath, not God's. The Jewish people forever remain God's prophetic time clock whose hands move only "when Israel is actually a nation." Ward further celebrated the fact that the United States stood ready to protect Israel.[33]

The 1956 *Pentecostal Evangel* indicated that the Suez crisis was a real danger. The troubles of national Israel would yield to a brighter future but only at the Second Coming.[34] Now the Israel-Arab conflict had "become a major world problem." Russia's lust for oil was bringing another looming crisis. Russia could invade Israel in pursuit of Haifa's oil pipeline from Iran. Israel needed God's intervention and protection.

After Israel's 1956 victory over Egypt, the 1957 *Pentecostal Evangel* expressed a new appreciation for Israel. It protested that many Pentecostals were unaware of the impressive message Israel offered the Church during the previous nine years. Pentecostals needed to better understand Israel's current significance. They needed to compare biblical prophecy with newspaper headlines. Israel was the only nation in history to "to experience a miraculous restoration of its autonomy." In spite of Arab or international antagonism, Israel would never be uprooted or scattered again.[35]

An editorial in the 1958 *Pentecostal Evangel* saw the 10th anniversary of Israel's national restoration as cause to celebrate its constant triumph over every fiery test. In spite of skeptics, Pentecostals needed to look beyond current passions in the Middle East and see Israel's restoration as part of the divine plan signaling the Second Coming.[36]

New outbreaks of anti-Semitism in 1960 in Moldovia, Ukraine, Russia, and even the United States dismayed the editor of the 1960 *Pentecostal Evangel.* He labeled synagogue and cemetery desecration and painted swastikas as "vicious, wicked, and intolerable." These were demonic attempts to destroy God's plan for the future when the Chosen People would play such a vital role. But God's intentions for a gloriously redeemed national Israel did not automatically result in salvation for all Jewish people. This is the reason for Assemblies of God Jewish missionary activities. Paul's compassion for Israel should be the Pentecostal's model.[37]

By 1965, the presses of the Assemblies of God appeared to sense pending war for Israel. Renewed Arab and terrorist threats seemed to call into question the viability for the continuance of the State of Israel without national spiritual transformation resulting from faith in Christ. Ultimately, Israel's perpetuity was guaranteed by God's promises. But Israel needed to focus on the Scriptures and repent more than they needed to irrigate, build factories and schools, or defend their borders.[38] Israel's 17th birthday was honored. But Pentecostals needed to continue praying for the salvation of the Jewish people.[39]

C.M. Ward wrote in 1966 that the Jewish people, the land, and national Israel were God's repository and fountain of all redemptive blessing. Calvary, the Bible, the Church, and Jesus Himself were all traced back to the Jewish Jerusalem fount. Jesus instructed His apostles to preach the Gospel to the Jewish people first, and thousands (literally, tens of thousands) of Jewish people did believe (see Acts 21:20). Israel was still a nation under contract with God. The Arab nations who surrounded Israel were a prime breeding ground for mischief and strife.[40] Plainly Ward assigned blame for the pending war on the Islamic world.

In honor of Israel's 19th anniversary of independence and on the eve of the 1967 Six Day War, the *Pentecostal Evangel* romantically recounted Ben

Gurion's 1948 announcement of Israel's statehood. It declared too that greater miracles than those in the Book of Acts awaited Jerusalem with the arrival of the King of kings.[41] The day before the Six Day War, it quipped that it might be correct to speak of "the Muddle East."

Egyptian President Nasser's aspirations for an empire included the destruction of Israel. Jordan's King Hussein signed on with Nasser in that quest. Perhaps the thwarting of the Jewish taking of Jerusalem was a sign that the Church had not fulfilled its mission to the Gentiles. Perhaps God was affording Christian missions an opportunity to complete the task.

The ramifications of the Six Day War were dramatic in their impact, even more so than the 1948 establishment of the State of Israel. It completely revitalized Pentecostal confidence in the perpetuity of national Israel. Former General Superintendent Riggs stated that God made a sevenfold covenant in the Pentateuch that Palestine would belong to the Jewish people forever. Twelve national sons of Ishmael had made war on Israel in June 1967, but Israeli victory against 20 to 1 odds confirmed God's giving Palestine to the Jewish people.[42] Once the Jewish people embraced Jesus, they would be in Zion forever. The 1960s Charismatic renewal was likewise proof that these are the last days.

C.M. Ward proclaimed that the newly liberated 20,000 square miles now under Israel's control had been authorized by Scripture. God's Word must prevail. When theocracy would be restored to Israel, even the deadness of the Dead Sea would be obliterated, and Israel's desert transformed into an Eden.[43]

However, 1969 was an epochal year in the Assemblies of God relations with Israel. Needing cash to purchase a building in Belgium, the Foreign Missions Department sold their only significant holding in the Holy City. This quiet sale of irretrievable property sold to the Greek Orthodox and resold to the Jewish Conservative Movement indicated Foreign Missions' despair of establishing any significant Jewish mission in Jerusalem. The tone of Pentecostal enthusiasm for the Jewish State significantly modified after 1969. Yet the eternal relationship between God and Israel could not be ignored. God and Israel were still inseparably bound together.[44]

Surprisingly, at the climax of Frank Boyd's life he was ready to move back in the direction of the Latter Rain restorationist positions of his forebears. Spirit-baptism was given to Jewish people in Acts 2 to equip them to carry the Gospel to all Gentile nations and bring them also into covenant relationship with God. Yet he insisted that the former and latter rains in biblical Israel made it clear there would be specific seasons for divine outpourings on Israel.[45]

Gordon Lindsay, who left the Assemblies of God to join independent faith healing ministries, wrote several popular books and pamphlets on Israel. He even endorsed his own daughter's conversion to Judaism and permanent move to Israel while retaining her faith in Jesus. But he ridiculed Christian enthusiasts for Israel who took no public stand on Israel's behalf. He actually became politically exercised in favor of Israel and in his disgust with infidel Arabs. He recognized an Israeli-Arab war was looming and called on Pentecostals to stand with Israel. Yet it remained clear that without Jesus, Israel could never become the people God wanted her to be.

NEW INTENSITY IN AMERICAN JEWISH MISSIONS

An appeal for funding Jewish evangelism was made in the 1950 *Pentecostal Evangel*. Missionary personnel were ready to preach "to the Jew first." In 1952, Jewish believers Charles and Jeannette Apton were appointed as field representatives to travel among Assemblies of God churches and encourage Jewish evangelism in local communities. An appeal was also made to support Jewish missionaries Meyer and Alice Tan-Ditter on the West Coast, home to a half million Jewish people. Their work was largely going door-to-door to thousands of Jewish homes.[46]

The Assemblies of God "Chicago Hebrew Mission" reported testimonies of visits to Jewish homes. Typically Jewish people were convinced that Jesus was the Messiah on the basis of Messianic prophecy, especially Isaiah 53. Wallace Bragg, pastor of Highway Tabernacle, wrote in 1954 of his congregation's desire to reach the 250,000 Jewish people of Philadelphia. Monty Garfield, an ordained Assemblies of God Jewish believer moved from San Diego to join in this effort. By this time the Assemblies of God had ten appointed missionaries working among the nearly 5.2 million American Jewish people representing nearly half the world's Jewish population.[47]

Ordained Jewish believer Ruth Specter complained in the 1957 *Pentecostal Evangel* that Pentecostals too often considered Israel as "subjects of prophecy" rather than people needing Christ. Just as early Jewish believers carried the good news to Gentiles, Gentiles should now energetically and sacrificially reciprocate. Evangelizing the Gentile world without evangelizing Jewish people was like a bird trying to fly with only one wing. Jewish believers had a history of becoming outstanding evangelists once they heard the Gospel. God was ready to extend mercy to a repentant Israel. Christians needed a baptism of love to scale the walls blocking Israel's spiritual freedom.[48]

The 1960 *Pentecostal Evangel* printed an interview with Dayton, Ohio, Jewish businessman, Nate Scharff. He declared that 97 percent of Jewish believers, including Scharff himself, were brought to Messianic faith by Gentile Christians.[49] In 1961, Ruth Witt Toczek of Chicago encouraged Pentecostals to believe for an avalanche of Jewish spiritual transformations before the Second Coming.[50]

Newly appointed Jewish missionary to Chicago Ernest Kalapathy wrote in the 1965 *Pentecostal Evangel* that the great hope for Israel must be her spiritual healing.[51] He noted in 1968 that new circles within Judaism were keen to enlighten ethics-depleted Gentiles with Jewish insight. How much greater should be the sense of Pentecostal duty toward the Jewish people. Woe to Christians who fail to preach Jesus![52]

The 1971 *Pentecostal Evangel* reported a recent "Jewish Evangelism Seminar" held in Springfield, Missouri, with most appointed missionaries present. They discussed preparation of new workers, development of evangelistic materials, Jewish evangelism seminars in local Assemblies, and training of Bible College students for Jewish ministry. Pentecostal interest in Jewish missions was on the rise.[53] Traditional Jewish opposition was lessening. More Jewish people were coming to Christ.

Chapter 6

PENTECOSTALISM'S ROMANTIC BREAKUP WITH ISRAEL:

Trial Separation or Divorce?

"There can be little dispute that the Pentecostal insurgence mushroomed into one of the most powerful religious upheavals of the twentieth century," declared Grant Wacker, historian at Duke Divinity School. In fact a 1979 Gallup poll found that 29 million Americans, 19 percent of all adults, considered themselves Pentecostal or Charismatic Christians.[1]

From the 1970s to the 1990s, new theologies were forming at the Pentecostal grassroots level as a result of theological borrowing among their growing ranks. This brought concern to Assemblies of God leaders. In a series of "position papers," they reaffirmed their commitment to teachings on miraculous healings, tongues-speaking as the initial evidence of the baptism in the Holy Spirit, and the divine covenant with Israel. By the late 1970s, widening diversity of opinion among constituents caused leaders conviction that Assemblies of God college faculties should fully subscribe to Assemblies of God positions including premillennial eschatology and the salvation of national Israel.

In 1979, the General Presbytery created a "Committee on Loopholes" to track sources of theological deviation. They found diversity. In addition to questions on the rapture and the inerrancy of Scripture, some even questioned tongues speaking as the initial evidence of Spirit-baptism and the role of Israel in the divine program.

A second report in 1981 urged local Assemblies of God district offices to more thoroughly examine those seeking ministerial credentials. New annual credential renewal forms required, among other issues, recommitment to tongues speaking as evidence of Spirit-baptism and premillennialism. By 1984, faculties were urged to use texts published by the Gospel Publishing House, the official Assemblies of God publishing arm, to assure student acceptance of classical Pentecostal positions.

The context of Pentecostalism was changing during the final three decades of the 20th century. Higher education became increasingly important. The number of college graduates tripled between 1960 and 1970.[2] Conservative political causes, such as moral values, creationism, school prayer, and national support for Israel remained strong. But personal religious comfort rather than eschatological tension was fostered. A new social casualness and a move away from Latter Rain restorationism gradually led to a lessening of Zionist sympathies.

Even as the Assemblies of God grew numerically and financially prospered in the 1980s and 1990s, the influx of new Charismatics impacted teaching on a variety of topics including the significance of Israel and her biblical destiny. The new tongues-speaking Charismatics came from denominations that dismissed the relevance of Israel in God's program. They supplemented the diluted support for Zionism and Israel. Assimilation into the larger American society further confused Pentecostal identity as many practices once condemned became socially palatable. But in the process, the Assemblies of God became broadly thought to be the world's largest Pentecostal denomination.[3] In reality, the predominantly African American Church of God in Christ (COGIC) is the single largest fellowship.

The October 1973 Yom Kippur War "wake-up call" sobered Pentecostals to realize Israel was not invincible. Astonished Pentecostals were disappointed at the shockingly opposite results of the Yom Kippur War to the very recent eschatologically stimulating 1967 Six Day War. Ideological room was made for Israeli vulnerability and potential defeat.

By 1982, the Assemblies of God determined to discontinue its political advocacy of Israel. The invasion of Lebanon brought extensive negative media portrayal of Israel's policies. The Assemblies of God also was expanding its interest in missions to the Islamic world. As a result, support for Zionism went missing in official Assemblies of God publications during the last two decades of the 20th century.

Supersessionist replacement theology, advocated by high profile Charismatics in the mid-1980s, caused a new Christian assault on the legitimacy of Israel's role in the divine economy. Bishop Earl Paulk of Atlanta, David Chilton of Texas, and others castigated Christian Zionism as misguided and dangerous. Several Assemblies of God voices reacted strongly against them.

Assemblies of God thinkers increasingly realized that dispensationalism militated against Pentecostal restorationism. Now they also realized that Charismatic replacement theory was a direct assault on both classical Pentecostal ideology and Israel's national legitimacy. Both dispensationalist and Charismatic camps threatened the survival of classical Pentecostalism and Zionism. The low ecclesiology of the dispensationalists and the widespread anti-Israelism of the Charismatic Movement should not be allowed to destroy the essence of Pentecostal ideology.

Those seeking to be politically correct attempted to separate the Assemblies of God from its ideological connection with the State of Israel in the mid-70s. Their attempt failed by the 1990s as Pentecostals found fresh motivations to renew their ideological bond.

YOM KIPPUR AND THE NEW ISRAELI REALITY
(1973–1981)

The lightning strikes of the Yom Kippur War had shocked most Americans and stunned Pentecostals. The feats of the Six Day War had seemed parallel to the deeds of biblical Israel. Inspired victories had seemed accompanied by angelic intervention on Israel's behalf. For an unprepared Israel to now have such a military setback staggered the faithful. Israel's ultimate respectable showing in the Yom Kippur War did not lessen the Pentecostal shock at Israel's vulnerability.

Those who feared for Israel's survival apart from national faith in Jesus saw the Yom Kippur War as indicative of the real potential for their worst fears for national Israel. Israel still stood defiant of God's truth. The Bible historically illustrated that God could call for Israel's national demise for unfaithfulness. Perhaps, as part of God's loving chastening, Israel would be in for protracted battle against her Islamic enemies. God was determined to have Israel embrace His Son, the Messiah.

Those motivated to reinforce dispensationalism's grip on the Assemblies of God constituency seized on Israel's misfortune to support Great Tribulation theories of massive Jewish suffering at the hands of the antichrist. But also, because Israel's near fate still seemed unknown, the Assemblies of God moved further away from its ideological identification with Israel and Zionism. It was content to focus on Israel's need for repentance and faith in Jesus and their eventual national exaltation at the Second Coming as fulfillment of prophecy. It did not want to be held accountable for pro-Zionist tendencies especially in the Islamic Middle East.

Meanwhile, Jewish evangelistic activities were fully endorsed. November 1973 marked a further turning point for Jewish missions. The concept of a Spirit-baptized Messianic synagogue was endorsed. Also an Assemblies of God National Jewish Committee was established; long support for ethnically diverse congregations made room for this. Congregations of Jewish believers could be fully immersed in a Jewish cultural frame. Thus, backing away from strong identification with the Jewish State was compensated for in Assemblies of God pathos for the ultimate redemption of Israel in Jesus.

In a surprisingly changed tone, the *Pentecostal Evangel* seemed to fault both sides in the Middle East conflict. Even C.M. Ward wrote, "When Israel learns of an impending enemy attack, she seizes the initiative and attacks first. This policy of preemptive strikes makes her a threat." Israel's growing isolation and perceived culpability would be further aggravated, as she would be blamed by Arab leaders for using refugees as political pawns.

The *Pentecostal Evangel* insisted that it was not in Israel's national interest to distort legitimate claims of the Palestinians. To rely on violence would only "tip the planet toward the chasm of nuclear holocaust." Yet it noted that a United Nations prejudice against Israel was nothing new.[4]

C.M. Ward warned in the 1977 *Pentecostal Evangel* that Jimmy Carter's administration's "human rights" campaign was "putting Israel on trial before a world forum" and invited Palestinians to pass judgment. He warned that OPEC nations could finance a prolonged war of attrition against Israel. He supported Menachem Begin's refusal to withdraw from the West Bank, and condemned Arafat's stubborn refusal to change course.[5]

Most Evangelical popularizers of eschatology saw no reason for Israeli compromise, since God was on Israel's side. They taught that the Arab-Israeli conflict would only cease in the millennium.[6] More liberal and pacifistic groups angrily disputed the notion that Israel's territorial expansion is foreordained. But neither Evangelicals nor Pentecostals put much stock in Jimmy Carter's sponsored 1978 Camp David Accords. Jerry Falwell stated, "There's not going to be any real peace in the Middle East until the Lord Jesus sits down upon the throne of David in Jerusalem."[7] In fact, Henry Kissinger's "shuttle diplomacy" earned him the epithet "antichrist" from many who saw him as an end-time counterfeit peacemaker.

Anti-Arab sentiment characterized much of premillennial teaching in the 1970s. Arab oil was seen as a weapon against Israel and the West in the antichrist's arsenal. But Israel's vulnerability provided Pentecostal leadership with a "reality check." It could make Pentecostalism's credibility equally vulnerable. To avoid the fate of a false prophet, appropriate action was needed to discretely inform Pentecostals of their need to distance themselves from Israel's potential disastrous fate. Their future and that of their children would be affected by what happens in Israel. Absent from current border disputes was any consideration of God's Word. Israel was "a seething cauldron of political intrigue and emotion."[8]

Unprepared Israel would have lost the Golan Heights had not the Syrians made serious blunders. Expressing fear for Israel's readiness for protracted warfare, the *Pentecostal Evangel* printed, "Israel has most to lose if a fifth Mideast war erupts."[9] Arab terrorism led Pentecostals to worry about Israel's troop demoralization as time and numbers were thought not to be on Israel's side. Israeli dynamiting of houses, arrests, and Arab deportations were also condemned.

C.M. Ward cautioned against running too fast in support of eschatological notions. With fewer than 200 Messianic Jewish believers among Israel's three million Jewish people, it was clear Israel was returning in continued unbelief. Developing into the people God wanted Israel to be might take another full generation.[10]

ISRAEL'S SUFFERING AND THE "CONVENIENCE" OF THE GREAT TRIBULATION

By World War II, the Assemblies of God had largely embraced the dispensational view of the Great Tribulation as a time for the antichrist's persecution of Israel. This was considered the key to Israel's national repentance and Messianic redemption. Such a tribulation, immediately preceded by the rapture of the Church into Heaven, was the vital bridge required to make dispensational's "kingdom delayed" theological system work. Most of the popular dispensational writers, however, were non-Pentecostal. Hal Lindsey's *The Late Great Planet Earth* reflected the views of Dallas Theological Seminary where Lindsey had studied.[11] His book took America by storm, selling 13 million copies in the 1970s and over 20 million by 1995.

Lindsey used Darby's dispensational system to link Scripture with current events. Israel's restoration in 1948 was the foremost sign of Christ's return. He conceived Matthew 23:36 to mean the Second Coming would occur with a 40-year generational lifespan. That is, around 1988. At last the pieces of the eschatological puzzle were coming together with Israel as the key. Soon Lindsey met with military planners in the American War College and the Pentagon to explain how Israel would be central to World War III. Israel's future opponents would include Russia, the Arabs, China, and the revived Roman Empire. Pentecostals consumed Lindsey's book. The *Pentecostal Evangel* emphasized the Great Tribulation as Jewish punishment and further strengthened the divide between Israel and the Church.

If Assemblies of God people ever recognized any man to be a prophet, it was David Wilkerson. He wrote in 1974 that Israel is invincible because it is flowing in the tide of divine prophecy.[12] The *Pentecostal Evangel* persisted in teaching that Israel would survive because she had a prophetic appointment with the antichrist to receive just retribution for her sins.[13] But Israel would still receive Jesus; consequently, she could not be annihilated.

OPPOSING VIEWS OF ISRAEL'S ROLE IN THE ENDTIMES

William Blackstone's book, *Jesus Is Coming*, published in 1889, sold about 700,000 copies over the next three decades. It awakened many conservative Protestants to keen interest in Zion. He held that hundreds of biblical prophecies proved that Israel would be restored to Zion. He also fought the amillennial position that Israel had been forever replaced by the Church in God's program. The Jewish people would yet receive their spiritual and temporal inheritance.

Reformed theologians disagreed. George Ladd of Fuller Theological Seminary said in 1978 that the New Testament shed no light on Israel as God's prophetic clock.[14] Catholic and Reformed theologians continued to allegorize prophetic passages, insisting that biblical promises to Israel as "My people" now applied only to Christian believers. God had no future for Israel apart from becoming Christians. Yet premillennialists still held to a literal interpretation of prophecy that called for a Jewish return to Zion. Evangelicals like Jerry Falwell insisted that national Israel existed in the will of God and functioned as the grandest witness to the pending Second Coming.[15]

One feature that continued from early dispensational eschatology was the idea of a Jewish antichrist. Second century Justin Martyr first suggested a Jewish antichrist from the tribe of Dan on the basis of the omission of Dan from the tribal list in Revelation 7. Popular acceptance of this contributed to outbreaks of European anti-Semitism. But the idea of a Jewish antichrist is entirely circumstantial and without any solid biblical basis.

ESCHATOLOGICAL ISRAEL IN ASSEMBLIES OF GOD IDEOLOGY

Alarmed by recent slippage in Christian support of modern Israel, C.M. Ward wrote *What You Should Know About Prophecy*. In it he declared that God's purposes for scattering Israel were to purify the Jewish people, not to destroy them. Israel's spiritual rebirth would now follow her political rebirth. But the 144,000 Spirit-filled, Spirit-led Messianic remnant of the Jewish people would perform their divine assignment during the Great Tribulation. This remnant of Israel would be Pentecostal, and the hovering Shechinah glory over Israel would signify God's presence among a changed Jewish people.[16]

Ward preached in 1976 that "the devil and the UN" did not appreciate God's everlasting promise to Israel. If one eliminated Israel's restoration, the Hebrew Bible was gone. The God who was so faithful to Abraham was neither arbitrary nor capricious and had never stopped loving Israel. God's gifts to Israel were granted without their merit and could not be revoked due to demerit.

Ward pointed out that "well-meaning folk like to feel that the failure of Israel has resulted in the blessings being transferred to us. The mistake is obvious...this contract is to be made with the physical descendants of Abraham and not with his spiritual seed." Ward, however, accepted the low ecclesiology of dispensationalism that the Church was only God's emergency provision established solely because of Israel's rejection of Jesus.[17]

GROWING PENTECOSTAL AWARENESS OF INCOMPATIBILITIES

There was a growing Pentecostal awareness of the incompatibilities between dispensationalism and Latter Rain restorationism. The fuller identification of Pentecostalism with Evangelicalism since the 1940s diminished its commitment to restorationism. Dispensational systems militated against the simpler restorationist expectation of a fully renewed and victorious Church prior to the Second Coming. This had the dramatic effect of lessening hopeful prospects for national Israel in the present time. Israel's redemption was not possible in dispensationalism without a seven-year tribulation period to bring it to repentance. Just as dispensationalism had a low ecclesiology, it had low expectations for impacting Israel for Kingdom good in the near future.

Charismatic Renewal—Foundation for Anti-Israelism

Vinson Synan wrote in 1993 that 19th-century British pastor, Edward Irving "became the first modern leader to challenge successfully the hold of 'cessationism' that had seeped into the churches since the time of St. Augustine." He also indicated that Catholic Pentecostals drew a clear line between themselves and earlier Protestant Pentecostals. The Catholic Charismatics traced their origin to John Paul XXIII's prayer that Vatican II (1962–1965) should be a "New Pentecost."[18]

By 1967, outpourings of the Spirit were occurring at Duquesne, Notre Dame, and other universities. Within months, a vital Charismatic movement functioned among priests, nuns, university professors, and students, as well as lay Catholics. They had differences with classical Pentecostals. They insisted tongues speaking was only one gift of several that may evidence Spirit-baptism. They clung to the power of Roman Church sacraments and maintained a strong Catholic identity. Instead of considering Spirit-baptism to be life-changing, they talked of a release of the Spirit. This allowed them to insist their Spirit-baptism experience was subsequent to their spiritual qualifications received through Roman rites of initiation.

However, the growing sense of new Charismatic liberties in the Charismatic renewal movement (CRM) and Catholic Charismatics caused many of them to join Assemblies of God churches, attend Assemblies of God colleges, and become ordained Assemblies of God ministers. In time, these new ministers would agree to the initial evidence teaching. Some, however, clung to their supersessionist or replacement theology leanings. To overcome criticism of spiritual elitism and factionalism, the Assemblies of God chose to quietly accommodate these replacement advocates rather than make Israel an in-house bone of contention.

Luther P. Gerlach's study on Pentecostalism showed Pentecostals were by now multi-generational and had wide-ranging personality profiles. Most notable were the high numbers of American youth. The new Charismatics either had no previous religious affiliation or were asked to leave the traditional churches after encouraging others to seek Spirit-baptism. Many Charismatics were in semi-autonomous cells that naturally divided and multiplied. They encouraged innovation, experimentation, and problem solving. Their wide range of styles enabled seekers to find a group most comfortable to them.[19]

These features went against the trend in the growingly centralized and structured Assemblies of God. Their leaders took positions on the local level to curtail "free-wheeling" Charismatics who gushed forth in personal prophecy to all comers. Many left, but those who did accept the more structured

Assemblies of God church existence stayed. But some brought their Christian anti-Semitism with them. Tongues as initial evidence could never be sacrificed without jeopardizing the reason for being of the Assemblies. But an anti-Israel position could be tolerated in the name of Christian unity since the main focus of Pentecostals is to transform people, not to change the social order.[20]

Traditional Pentecostal premillennialists clung to the bedrock truth of a covenant-keeping God who would never go back on His promises to the patriarchs. But dispensationalism left them in a double-minded vice. Early century restorationism anticipated a glorious crescendo of divine activity in Israel that would quickly lead to the Messianic kingdom. But the adopted dispensationalism required more Jewish suffering for its system to logically function. The ambiguity and tension between the two systems forced an eventual shutdown of discussion of Israel as a political topic in Assemblies of God periodicals.

Derek Prince, a Charismatic prophetic spokesman, stated of Israel's sufferings that God permits suffering for those He loves because it is the only way the valuable end result can be achieved.[21] Chuck Smith, founder of the Spirit-filled Calvary Chapel network, indicated God is calling Israel to come out of the commercial Wall Street system. Merrill Unger, the prolific biblical scholar, believed the Jewish people will be changed from their unbelieving Jacob role to being Israel, a prince with God.[22]

Yet several leading Pentecostals and Evangelicals considered continuing American support for Israel after the Yom Kippur War to be of paramount importance. C.M. Ward indicated in 1974 that Jewish people were discovering the role Jesus Christ was playing in that crisis. Israeli eyes were seeing America as a Christian nation that alone came to their aid in the Yom Kippur War.

In a spirit the Assemblies of God Pentecostals could identify with, Jerry Falwell, founder of the Moral Majority, indicated in 1985 that the United States would lose its importance to God if it failed to protect Israel. Every Christian had an obligation to support Israel.[23] Author Hal Lindsey believed that if the U.S. turned its back on Israel it would no longer exist as a nation.[24]

Nationally known Bible teacher Tim LaHaye insisted that Jewish people should realize that "Bible-believing, premillennial Christians are Israel's best friends."[25]

THE HOLY SPIRIT AND ISRAEL

Pentecostals continued to value reports of Pentecostal activities among Jewish people as further confirmation of the Latter Rain connection with Zion. As late as 1972, a medical doctor, W. Douglas Fowler Jr. of Jacksonville, Florida, wrote the editor of the New Wine magazine to report a miraculous speaking in tongues in Hebrew to an American Jewess while driving from Jacksonville to Mobile. His message was totally unintelligible to him. But the Jewess translated it and understood it to be a message from God to her.

The one leading Pentecostal personality the Israeli government chose to court was Oral Roberts. After his all-paid trip to Israel in 1967 and his meeting with high government officials, he wrote, "God's ancient people are carving out an empire. That's what the Bible told us they would do. The meaning of this in terms of a coming great world revival and the Second Coming of Jesus has thrilled me to the very fiber and core of my being."[26]

Classical Pentecostals would never entirely escape that restoration bond of the Spirit they enjoyed with Israel. In the highest Pentecostal academic arena, the Society for Pentecostal Studies, or in the exchange forum of *Paraclete* magazine, leading Assemblies of God theologians like Stanley Horton and academics like Amos Millard in the later 1970s, celebrated the eternal Pentecostal bond with the ultimately Spirit-filled nation of Israel.

Stanley Horton wrote for *Paraclete* in 1977, emphasizing that the same work of the Spirit Pentecostals presently enjoyed would likewise benefit Israel:

> God did warn Israel that if they became disobedient...He would use other nations to punish them and scatter them (Deuteronomy 28:36,37,64,65). *But God did not mean to retract His promise to Abraham* concerning the land.[27] [My emphasis.]

Many are still scattered. Thus the final restoration...implies no more judgment on Israel because of *the outpouring of God's Spirit upon them*....It is evident therefore that Revelation 20 does give us a place where the restoration of Israel to the land will be brought to its climax *by the outpouring of God's Spirit* on restored and repentant People. *He will yet put His Spirit within them.*[28] [My emphasis.]

Amos Millard wrote in 1978 for *Paraclete* of the mutual reliance of Pentecostals and Israel on the passage, "Not by might, nor by power, but by my Spirit, saith the Lord" (see Zech. 4:6). This biblical passage appeared both on the cover of the *Pentecostal Evangel* and beneath the Menorah at the Israeli Knesset. Millard proclaimed that the answer to Israel's dilemmas was the *supernatural power and direct intervention of the Holy Spirit.* When the Messiah would come, *"all in Israel...would be recipients of the poured-out Spirit...the Holy Spirit is the instrument in the regathering and restoration of Israel to the land,"* as well as to fellowship with God and anointing for world service...after her *enduement with the outpoured Spirit.*[29] (My emphasis.)

These scholars proclaimed afresh what classical Pentecostals believed from the inception of the movement. A restored Israel and a restored Church would be equally dependent on and energized by the same Holy Spirit. The Spirit was restoring both camps to their former glory and usefulness to the King of kings.

RENEWED STRATEGIES FOR ASSEMBLIES OF GOD JEWISH MISSIONS

A combination of new realities in 1973 compelled the Assemblies of God to rethink its mission strategy among the Jewish people in the United States. The Department of Home Missions had officially appointed Jewish missionaries to American cities since 1945, but a new aggressiveness was birthed after the Yom Kippur War.

The Charismatic Renewal Movement (CRM) and the related Jesus move-ment of the late 1960s and early 1970s caused thousands of Jewish people to suddenly surface in Pentecostal congregationas. From across the broadened Assemblies of God constituency came accusations of bureaucratic shortsight-edness on the basis of the ill-advised 1969 sale of the greatly needed and sole Assemblies of God property in Jerusalem. The General Council was ready to look for ways to demonstrate goodwill toward Jewish ministry and somehow redeem its tarnished image.

Although Israeli historian Yaakov Ariel classified the Jesus People as one of several groups seeking spiritual experiences, thousands of Jewish Jesus people were among them.[30] Fellow travelers were persuaded of the active participation of multiplied thousands of Spirit-baptized Jewish youth fully committed to Jesus and the Pentecostal experience. Assemblies of God circles made efforts to incorporate them.

However, the single largest reason for Assemblies of God willingness to explore new avenues of Jewish mission was the growing effectiveness of their Jewish missions. Hundreds of new Jewish believers in Los Angeles, St. Louis, Fort Lauderdale, and elsewhere were impressive. It seemed the ultimate Jew-ish awakening to Christ could be at hand. It seemed Pentecostals who worked in signs, wonders, and miracles were the very people God might use to most greatly impact American Jewry.

The national Assemblies of God seminar on Jewish evangelism in 1973 adopted recommendations for continuation of Jewish ministry, the appoint-ment of a National Jewish Committee, the initiation of training for Jewish evangelism in Bible schools, and increased promotion of Jewish ministry in Assemblies of God publications.[31] But the most significant outcome of the 1973 seminar was the authorization to establish Pentecostal Messianic syna-gogues. The missionaries were pragmatically told to find "what works."

Unknown to the Assemblies of God personnel at the time, two other independent Messianic synagogues had just opened in Cincinnati, Ohio, and

Gaithersburg, Maryland. Also unknown was the fact that New York City had hosted seven Messianic synagogues early in the 20th century. The Pentecostal missionaries naively imagined in 1973 they were to pioneer the first Messianic synagogues since the Book of Acts.

Ernest Kalapathy, Jewish missionary in Chicago, wrote in the 1973 *Pentecostal Evangel* that conditions that prevailed in the 1st century were beginning to be the case again today. He admitted the continued dominant Jewish rejection of Christ but believed the Jewish believing minority was a growing remnant.[32]

The 1974 Jewish Leadership Seminar was filled with optimism. It introduced Philip Goble's initial draft of his book, *Everything You Need to Grow a Messianic Synagogue*, as a manual for establishing indigenous Jewish congregations.

With Jewish people responding in such numbers, the 1975 *Pentecostal Evangel* called for spiritual revival that would shake Jewish communities, and declared that Messianic Jewish people would be used of God to exalt the name of Jesus. Then the 1975 annual Jewish Seminar proposed four projects: (1) Preparation of a correspondence course to train Gentiles to reach Jewish people; (2) Development of a family life program and the preparation of literature for Jewish children; (3) Adaptation of Jewish tracts and a study course for Jewish deaf people and Braille literature for the Jewish blind; and (4) Preparation of films and slide presentations for promotions, education, and evangelism.[33]

The 1978 *Pentecostal Evangel* reported that many scores of new Jewish believers had accepted Christ and been immersed in water as seen at Temple Beth Emanuel (later *Ahavat Zion*) in Los Angeles. Hebrew language and bar and bat mitzvah classes as well as Jewish weddings were being conducted in new Messianic synagogues.[34] The 1979 Assemblies of God Jewish Conference called for wider denominational participation in Jewish evangelism and the proper equipping of all involved.

The *Pentecostal Evangel* noted "great sensitivity to the spiritual needs of American Jewish people" among Assemblies of God Bible college students. Scores were called to Jewish ministry but needed equipping. The new Jewish studies program for that purpose was developing at Valley Forge Christian College in Phoenixville, Pennsylvania.[35]

Ten Central Bible College students traveled to New York in 1981 and met with the director of Inter-Faith Relations of the Anti-Defamation League, Rabbi Solomon Bernards. He encouraged them to be a witness and show what they stood for by how they lived.[36]

All the while, the Assemblies of God made much of its distribution of the New Testament in Israel. Later, it noted that the Israeli government was taking steps to prevent the free distribution of Bibles in the Israel school system that included the New Testament. But one Israeli government authority assured Assemblies of God officials touring Israel that the new "anti-missionary" law passed by the Knesset did not target Christian missionary work.

NEW PENTECOSTALISM CHALLENGES (1982–1989)

In 1982, David Irwin, missions professor at the Assemblies of God Theological Seminary, established the Center for Muslim Ministry. With this, the Division of Foreign Missions embraced a challenge to create Pentecostal awareness of one billion unevangelized Muslims. With this new focus on Muslims, the focus on Jewish evangelism dramatically lessened. Between 1982 and 1989 there were only 13 articles relative to Jewish missions in the *Pentecostal Evangel.*

The high profile given to the Center for Muslim Evangelism from 1982 onward was due in part to the events and decisions taken in the Islamic world. American sympathies were growing for victims of human rights abuses as suffered by Muslim masses at the hands of Islamic regimes. At the same time, the American media was controlled by those seeking to drive a wedge between Americans and their historically favorable Zionist leanings.

The Israeli 1982 invasion of Lebanon, in hot pursuit of Yasser Arafat and his PLO terrorists, enjoyed initial American sympathies. But the slaughter of hundreds of Palestinians by Lebanese tribal groups later horrified them. David

Lewis, Assemblies of God prophecy evangelist and author, argued that Israel had delayed Russia's invasion of the Middle East by her police action in Lebanon.[37] Grant Jeffrey, a Pentecostal Canadian author, documented that Israel's defensive action taken in Lebanon had uncovered stockpiles of Russian arms including tanks, anti-tank missiles, thousands of shells, hundreds of thousands of uniforms, AK-47 assault rifles, and millions of rounds of ammunition. The K food rations found had a shelf life of only six months, indicating that a massive attack on Israel was planned for the fall of 1982.[38] Israel's defensive action in Lebanon, therefore, was more than justified.

These facts convinced true believers, but many were uncertain. On the heels of the invasion of Lebanon came the bombing of the American military base in Beirut in October 1983 when 241 Americans died. This, combined with other events, caused many Americans to question American policy toward Israel. The changing political sentiment in turn impacted evangelistic sympathies. Nothing could have been better for sensing the need for the Center for Muslim Ministries or worse for Assemblies of God Jewish evangelism.

The restorationist vision of Pentecostalism seemed more unlikely of fulfillment with every new political dilemma, economic setback, or military crisis. An anemic dispensationalist ecclesiology spawned, fostered and reinforced the lowered expectations for church accomplishment in the here and now. New strong and optimistic voices of protest arose in both Charismatic and Assemblies of God circles.

PENTECOSTAL EVANGELISTIC CHALLENGES

David Barrett, research consultant for both the Southern Baptists and the Vatican, estimated that in 1988 there were 360 million Pentecostals and Charismatics representing 21 percent of the world's Christians. He projected some 560 million by 2000. John Naisbitt, also in 1988, noted that many conservative denominations had doubled since 1965. Jehovah's Witnesses rose from

330,000 to 752,000, and Seventh-day Adventists from 365,000 to 666,000. But Assemblies of God quadrupled from 572,000 to 2.1 million.[39]

Thomas Zimmerman, General Superintendent of the Assemblies of God in 1981, claimed that Pentecostalism is in the mainstream of theological orthodoxy. Margaret Poloma, in *The Assemblies of God at the Crossroads: Charisma and Institutional Dilemmas* (1989), claimed that the Assemblies of God would continue giving verbal support to Charismatics while aligning more and more with Evangelical denominations. It would also blend more and more with biblically uninformed American society.[40] These realities would generate the Assemblies of God yet further distancing itself from its earlier pro-Israel position.

The marriage of Pentecostalism and Evangelicalism had communal imaging benefits. The influx of the middle class in the 1970s and 1980s improved the Assemblies of God public image in local communities. Robert Cooley was elected president of Gordon-Conwell Theological Seminary. Russell Spittler served as administrator, faculty member, and later provost at Fuller Seminary. Thomas Zimmerman and Donald Argue served as presidents of the National Association of Evangelicals. The Assemblies of God took pride in the Evangelical acceptance of such Assemblies of God leaders.

It should be noted, however, that Assemblies of God leadership did not flock to right-wing causes but rather tended to avoid public issues including international affairs. Yet by 1989 the General Council in session took the bold step of acknowledging racism as sin against Jewish people, Arabs, and Africans in particular.

Avoidance of political issues did not prevent protest against anti-Semitism. The *Pentecostal Evangel* reported a doubling of anti-Semitism in the United States between 1979 and 1980.[41] Many evangelicals, however, replaced anti-Semitism with anti-Zionism. Harold Lindsell, editor of *Christianity Today* from 1968 to 1978, indicated in 1984 that biblical adherence to the ultimate Jewish destiny should not prevent Christian witness of the plight of the Arabs. Mark Hanna, Evangelical professor at Talbot Seminary callously published, "We are not told in the New Testament to pray for the peace of Jerusalem....We must not forget...the many thousands of Arab Christians who are part of the body of Christ and so related to us by a spiritual bond that can never be matched by the historical ties of Israel to the West and to the church."[42] But this type of anti-Zionist, anti-Israel attack would not characterize Assemblies of God publications at all—in spite of the increasing tendency to identify with Evangelical trends.

EVANGELICAL GREAT TRIBULATIONISM

Gershon Greenberg, professor at American University and specialist on Christian attitudes toward Israel, feared a potential eruption of Christian anti-Zionism when the Second Coming did not materialize in time. But the dispensationalist dogma allowed for both ongoing pro-Zionism and disappointment with Israel's continued rejection of Jesus. Prior to the rapture, Israel could only be expected to remain Gospel resistant. Evangelicals tended to emphasize the Great Tribulation as necessary to bring Israel to Christ.

Pentecostals regularly watched Jack Van Impe on television. He seemed to readily accept that a "wave of anti-Semitism will sweep the earth" as part of *Israel's Final Holocaust*. Van Impe still professed love for the Jewish people but said God would "permit Satan one last attempt to murder every Jew upon the face of the earth."[43]

Dwight Wilson, a historian with deep Assemblies of God roots, protested against the Pentecostalist tendency to pique eschatological enthusiasm. He faulted Pentecostals for having considered the 1956 Israeli attack·on Egypt to be part of the divine plan that would lead to Russian invasion of Israel and Armageddon. Wilson also accused Pentecostals of "cavalier treatment toward Muslim interests" as they consistently sided with the Jewish people. He further objected to Pentecostal participation in Christian lobbies on Israel's behalf and their sending money to support Jewish settlements in the West Bank.[44]

PENTECOSTALS "ON BEHALF OF ISRAEL" IN THE 1980S

Many Israeli leaders defended courting of Evangelicals on pragmatic grounds. Israel's prime ministers from David Ben Gurion to Ehud Barak and Benjamin Netanyahu all appreciated Evangelical Christian support of Israel.

The *Pentecostal Evangel* twice reported its concern in 1981 that increasing Israeli immigration to the West was endangering the welfare of the State of Israel. It quoted Helen Wolfer of the *Jerusalem Post*, "Evidently the younger generation in Israel has lost sight of the romanticized ideal.... The emigrants are not willing to make the sacrifices the early Zionists made."[45]

David Wilkerson, internationally renowned evangelist, wrote that judgment awaited America in spite of her defense of Israel. "God will protect Israel and send fire on us! ...The defense of Israel will not be our battle but the Lord's—so that Israel will give all glory to God."[46]

Dan Betzer, pastor and radio evangelist for Revivaltime, wrote several books for distribution to his national radio audience. All of them complied with standard premillennial dispensationalism. His importance in relationship to Israel was his strong advocacy of Israel's right to exist. One of his chief concerns was combating supersessionist "replacement theology."

As a pastor, Betzer had sponsored Freda Keet, a non-religious Israeli, for speaking tours. He hoped she would foster faith in the Abrahamic covenant in a time of intense international anti-Zionist propaganda sponsored by the OPEC nations. The Assemblies of God churches enthusiastically embraced the Israeli spokeswoman. She was deeply moved.[47]

The *Pentecostal Evangel* highlighted the 1981 efforts of Mike Evans to spearhead a special observance for Israel's 33rd birthday at the Alabama governor's mansion. Governor Fob James hosted the event. Alabama was the first state to issue a proclamation of blessing to celebrate Israel's independence.[48] Evans, in 1983, revealed his own intense involvements in both Israeli and American political arenas for their mutual benefit.

NEW DANGERS TO THE PENTECOSTAL IDEOLOGY OF ISRAEL

The Assemblies of God realized by the 1980s that the Charismatic numbers were too vast to ignore. Coveting their church memberships, many determined to increase their rosters by an open-arm policy toward the Charismatic groups. Much of the excessive informality and normal Charismatic participation in "worldly" habits and events initially bothered classical Pentecostals. But the amazing multiplication of Charismatic congregations to between 40,000 and 60,000 by 1989 demonstrated the folly of rigid religion. A second concern was that a host of newly created and flourishing Charismatic denominations were siphoning off excessive numbers of classical Pentecostals.

The early Pentecostal virtues of humility, gentleness, and love were replaced by Charismatic boasts of dominion and authority. The Charismatic image of God was often viewed in a mirror reflecting the American materialistic way of life. Responsibility for the common good was abandoned for selfish personal interests. The Assemblies of God was increasingly impacted by the attitudes of secular America. For example, many viewed glossolalia or tongues speaking as "my prayer language" instead of empowerment for evangelistic witness. Therefore, any significance of tongues speaking in relation to eschatological restorationism was lost. With it went the connection between Pentecostal experience and Zionism.

KINGDOM NOW AND DOMINION ANTI-ZIONISM

A sizeable outgrowth of the Charismatic Movement was the "Kingdom Now" or "Dominion" phenomenon. This was primarily the product of Atlanta pastor, Earl Paulk. To eliminate eschatological significance to biblical passages, he allegorized them, giving a mystical significance only. He believed Israel does not have a future different from any other nation. Many now believed that the grassroots support of Israel would change within decades.

One anonymous leader agreed that "Christianity has superseded Judaism, and the Church is now God's covenant community…and Judaism has no more validity than Islam."[49] David Chilton, a leading proponent of dominionism, taught that the Bible does not indicate that God has any future plan for Israel.[50] He also declared that the god of Judaism is the devil, and that Christian Zionism is blasphemy. Another leader pronounced judgment on Israel as a "sinful, apostate, Christ-rejecting, blasphemous Middle East nation."[51]

DEFENSE OF ISRAEL AND IDEOLOGICAL RESURGENCE

The 1987 Presbytery of the Assemblies of God perceived the dangers of Kingdom Now doctrine. In answer, they adopted a white paper entitled, "A Summary of Some Kingdom Now Doctrines Which Differ From the Teaching of the Assemblies of God." It recognized that the Kingdom Now doctrine advocates spiritualized Scripture to support their theories. The position that God's covenant with Israel has been abrogated occurs in various places in their writings.

In the face of extremist Kingdom Now ideology, the Assemblies of God was soon compelled to recognize its own need to recall its earlier roots. In the early 1900s, Pentecostals recognized their movement to be the divinely reestablished apostolic Christianity at the climax of salvation history "to manifest the glory of the Latter Rain."[52] Over time, the gradual muting of the apocalyptic vision made holiness "separation from the world" appear quaint and pointless to newer members. They forgot to what extent early beliefs provided them with their group sense of eternal value.

Calls were heard for new Pentecostal theologies. Pentecostals recognized their need to walk in the fullness of the Latter Rain heritage here and now. In keeping with this new awakening, Amos Millard, at the 1983 annual meeting of the Society for Pentecostal Studies, stated,

> God...has declared His purpose to restore both natural and spiritual Israel. In essence, this is what the Pentecostal movement is all about! It is not a coincidence that in the same era that Israel is being restored...the Church is being restored to the spiritual power and resources it once knew in its apostolic history.[53] [My emphasis.]

The tremendously bad American press given to Israel with the beginning of the Intifada in 1987 generated widespread negativity toward Israel. Even Jewish American notables like Woody Allen led nationally published Jewish attacks on Israel's treatment of Palestinians. But the Assemblies of God chose to stay out of the political fray to avoid appearances of political favoritism and did not address the issue.

PENTECOSTAL REEXAMINATION OF ZIONISM AND THE STATE OF ISRAEL (1990-1999)

The sheer weight of Pentecostal and Charismatic numbers throughout the world highlight their importance to the 21st century. It is imperative to understand the issues they face as they consider the one people they can never avoid: the Jewish people. Biblically intense Pentecostals confront the Jewish reality every day even in their private spiritual pursuits. There can be no doubt that whatever their varieties or views, Pentecostals are and will be a powerful force in world opinion throughout the 21st century. The last decade of the 20th century offered brighter prospects for Pentecostal ideology.

Dispensationalism was losing much of its appeal in 1989 and 1990. The rapid transformation of Eastern Europe was inconsistent with its popularized version that had pictured a very different outcome. But Saddam Hussein's Iraqi invasion of Kuwait in August 1990 suddenly reopened the ravenous appetites of prophecy buffs. Hal Lindsey's *The Late Great Planet Earth* shot up in sales 83 percent. The peril Israel now faced as nations gathered for war within striking distance of Jerusalem appealed to American readership. Surely the end was at hand as the world readied for battle at Megiddo.

Timothy Weber, esteemed American Church historian, noted in 1990 that even dispensationalists out of Dallas Theological Seminary had begun to modify elements of the dispensationalist scheme. These revisions included the "Kingdom delayed" or postponement theory and the absolute divorce of Israel and the Church.[54] Within five years, Stanley Horton, never a dispensationalist anyway, wrote, "Clearly, God will be faithful to His promises to national Israel without splitting Israel and the Church into two people and two plans. To accept this, many dispensationalists today have modified the classic dispensational view."[55]

Academic Pentecostal circles were recognizing that dispensationalism was incompatible with Pentecostal distinctives. Grant McClung of the Church of God (Cleveland, Tennessee) wrote in 1990, "The theological story of mainline North American Pentecostalism still has too much of an evangelical accent and needs to be rediscovered in a fresh Pentecostal/charismatic hermeneutic."[56] James K.A. Smith of Villanova University wrote in 1997 that, in the light of Evangelical hermeneutic that precludes the Pentecostal experience, "If our theology is to be Pentecostal, I think it is crucial that we give up trying to be evangelical, or at least evangelical theologians."[57]

Consistent with the original Pentecostalist restorationism, Gordon Anderson, president of North Central University wrote in 1994,

> Pentecostals see God acting continuously throughout the Church Age in the same way as He did in the Book of Acts.... Pentecostals believe in a baptism of the Holy Spirit that empowers people for service, as in the Early Church....God does miracles today and...the Holy Spirit...is the agent in

the life of the believer by which these miracles occur....In this respect Pentecostals are nondispensational.[58]

Accordingly, Pentecostal perspective needed to retain Israel as an integral part of the divine program in the present. Therefore, Stanley Horton could write the following in 1996:

> Jesus looked ahead to a spiritual restoration of the people of Israel....It is true that both the Old and New Testaments show that Gentile believers will share with Israel in the future glories of the Messiah's reign. But this does not mean the Church replaces Israel....The Bible again and again declares that God will reveal Himself in connection with His dealings with the nation of Israel....The promise of their restoration is unconditional...He will make Israel a blessing to us all during the Millennium."[59]

Horton looked forward to Israel's blessing during the earthly reign of the Messiah. But he did not support abandonment of Jewish evangelism in the present. He wrote,

> The future miraculous salvation of Israel, however, does not mean that we should neglect seeking salvation of Jews today.... Therefore, even though some Jews rejected Jesus, Jesus did not reject Israel as a nation....His faithfulness would also be seen in giving them a new heart and a new spirit and in putting His Spirit within them (Ezek. 36:26-27; 37:14).[60]

PENTECOSTAL IDEOLOGY OF ISRAEL AT THE CONSUMER LEVEL

The battle for the minds of Pentecostals was not to be fought only at higher academic levels but on the grassroots level as well. Pentecostal bookstores continued to sell paperbacks featuring their entire prophetic schemes on the dispensational foundation. Especially dangerous were infidel Christians who taught that Jewish people really did not need Jesus but had a separate covenant that gave them an eternally Christ-less relationship with God. The *Pentecostal Evangel* protested that "in the guise of friendship the promoters of the dual covenant theology withhold the gospel from the Jewish people. They deny the desire of the King of the Jews for His own people."

STRONG POLITICAL STAND FOR ISRAEL

Fear of harming their missions interests or causing the deaths of missions personnel in Islamic countries made the Assemblies of God no longer want to be publicly identified with Zionist causes. The best the *Pentecostal Evangel* could muster was a citation of Jewish accomplishments and contributions to the betterment of humankind—with the adage, "The Jewish people are not perfect, but they deserve a place of honor in the annals of human history."[61]

Yet most Pentecostals believed America's welfare was dependent on her treatment of Israel. After citing the history of Christian Zionism, J.R. Church expressed his growing anxiety in 1995 at the mounting American political reluctance to unreservedly support Israel. He said Arab oil had been used to blackmail the United States, and he appealed to international self-interest as Christians and nations stood to benefit from Israel's fulfilled destiny. In fact, if Israel could presently enter her full inheritance, all nations could benefit.[62]

Professor Dwight Wilson of Bethany College, former critic of support of Israel, pointed out in 1988 that the Pentecostal view of "the outpouring of the Spirit as itself a fulfillment of end-time prophecy" had become the sole distinction between Pentecostal and fundamentalist eschatologies. He also recognized that early Pentecostals felt a family connection with Zionists and a certain partnership in restorationism.[63]

Meanwhile, Yaakov Ariel wrote in 1993 that the Israeli government did not grasp the roots and motivations of Christian Zionists. The Israeli government likewise did not believe Christian missionaries could be a threat to Jewish religion.[64] Every prime minister since Ben Gurion repeatedly met with American Evangelical organizations and leading Christian personalities to foster improved relations and political goodwill. Assemblies of God evangelists David Lewis, Mike Evans, and Canadian-born Grant Jeffrey all had extensive political involvements with Israeli government leaders and used those regular contacts to promote pro-Israel causes in the Pentecostal world.

David Lewis enjoyed a regular history of interactions with prime ministers and other high officials over three decades. He widely disseminated pro-Israel information through his publications. Based in Springfield, Missouri, he served as something of an "in-house conscience" of the Assemblies of God executives concerning Israel. He enjoyed broad-based support among Assemblies of God pastors and laymen alike. God's favor on Zion and the Jewish people was his constant theme. Never engaging in Jewish evangelism, he deliberately preserved his credentials among Jewish leaders and Israeli government officials.

Lewis wrote prolifically on biblical prophecy. He highlighted Christian responsibility to maintain a gracious and faithful attitude toward Israel and the Jewish people. He declared that every Christian who embraced biblical Zionism expressed his faith in God and God's Word. Christians had the duty to love Israel unconditionally, that is, without any evangelistic agenda.[65]

Lewis called for Pentecostal pulpits to take a bold stand against anti-Semitism. He contended that the fate of both Israel and all Evangelical churches was at stake since satan desired the destruction of both.

Michael D. Evans, a long-term Assemblies of God Jewish evangelist, became a political advocate for Israel. He had regular audiences with every prime minister since Menachem Begin. He argued for Israel's right to secure borders, reported on Israel's state of military preparedness, advocated removal of the American embassy to Jerusalem, protested United Nations abuse of

Israel, and shared human interest stories of modern Jewish refugees returning to Israel. He sponsored a number of national conferences and produced several nationally viewed prime time television specials to promote Christian support for Israel. He has been honored in numerous ways by Israeli government officialdom for his tireless efforts on Israel's behalf.

Grant Jeffrey was ordained with the Pentecostal Assemblies of Canada. His many books on prophecy fostered much goodwill toward Israel in the United States as well as Canada. He denounced business cooperation with the Arab boycott of Israel. He protested hatred for Israel manifested in unbalanced media reporting on the Middle East and the United Nations' treatment of Israel. Arab governments were cynically using Palestinians in their war on Israel while abusing Palestinians within their own borders.[66]

Jeffrey erred on two important counts, however. He presumed the antichrist to be Jewish. He also mistook Chabad Lubavitcher signs in Jerusalem reading, "We want Messiah Now!" as reflecting the general Israeli disposition. Both issues misled his extensive readership.

RESTORATIONIST REVIVAL AND NEW HOPE FOR ISRAEL

The growing distrust of dispensationalism in Pentecostal academic circles, especially in the 1990s, encouraged a reexamination of the restorationist ideology of early 20th-century Pentecostalism. This had direct bearing on Pentecostal optimism for Israel and provided new motivation for Zionist causes.

A new look at restorationism in the 1990s challenged afresh the classical Christian tenet that the charismata ceased at the end of the apostolic 1st century. Challenged also was the theologically rendered thought that Israel was essentially useless to God beyond the 1st century date. Both 1st-century apostolic Christian and Jewish nationhood needed revitalization in modern times for God's plan for the ages to properly culminate.

In the face then of the dire formulas for Israel offered by dispensational-ism and the postmillennial dismissal of Israel in Kingdom Now teachings, the Assemblies of God Pentecostal Textbook Project published *Bible Doctrines* in 1994. Under a section entitled, "God's Promises to National Israel," William Menzies and Stanley Horton wrote,

> The land was also an integral part of the promise to Abraham and to Israel. ... He will live up to His Name; He will be the kind of faithful God He says He is. God is going to restore Israel both materially and spiritually even though they have profaned His holy Name. He will do it to honor His holy Name, that is, to demonstrate His holy nature and character.

> [Romans 11:1] makes it clear that God has not thrown aside His people! The context shows the Bible is talking about lit-eral, national Israel and shows that God has not changed His mind about His promises.[67]

After describing errors in postmillennialist Kingdom Now thinking, Hor-ton wrote,

> They ignore the many Scripture passages that show God still has a purpose for national Israel in His plan.[68]

> Israel, restored, cleansed, filled with God's Holy Spirit, will undoubtedly occupy all the land promised to Abraham (Gen. 15:18). In the Millennium...Israel and the church are in fact one people of God...one by faith in Christ and common partaking of the Spirit, and yet distinct insofar as God will yet restore Israel as a nation to its land...[under] One new covenant.[69]

Horton was confident of the work of the Holy Spirit upon Israel both in the present and future. Without denying the ultimate victory of Israel in the millennium, he wrote,

> The people of the restored Israel will also be filled with the Spirit.... Joel 2:28 shows a continuing outpouring, not just on the Day of Pentecost, but on "all flesh": (Heb. *kol basar*).... Because of the multitude of Israel... are transformed, the Holy Spirit's work in the Millennium will be more powerful and more wonderful than ever...We have a first installment of this now, but then we shall enjoy a greater fullness in connection with the Lord's return and the restoration of Israel in the land.[70]

Plainly, Horton believed Israel needed to embrace Christ and was confident this would be the ultimate reality. But Horton's national Israel is not the rag-tag group of Jewish survivors who manage to live to tell the tale of all the horrors of dispensationlism's Great Tribulation, a "second Holocaust." His national Israel gladly embraces Jesus and immediately enters into the full measure of God's promises on all counts. The onus, from Horton's point of view, would be on Pentecostals not to idly wait in fateful anticipation of more Jewish tragedy, but rather to actively encourage Jewish faith now with the loving Christian hope all future Jewish tragedy could be entirely averted. Christian success at provoking national Israel to spiritual jealousy, with the resultant positive Jewish faith response, would immediately evoke the Second Coming and the implementation of all biblical promises for national Israel.

THE SECOND MILLENNIUM CLIMAX OF ASSEMBLIES OF GOD JEWISH EVANGELISM

My thorough search of Assemblies of God Gospel Publishing House adult educational materials from 1973 through 1985 astonishingly revealed only two mentions of the State of Israel.[71] One read,

For a thousand years before the return of Jews to Israel in this century, such a return did seem impossible. Since May 14, 1948, the dream has become a reality....God is doing his work. Resistance to Christ is still strong in the land, but there is a nucleus of believers. We must recognize, however, that *God is not in a hurry....The sufferings of the Jews are not over yet,* but God will be faithful. As Christians we can take courage, for we see these things as signs of Christ's soon return. [My emphasis.]

The scarcity of reference to Israel suggests the thought of the national salvation of Israel had become irrelevant to biblical studies. All told, the period of 1973 to 1999 was not comparable to the keen interest and frequent optimism exhibited by Pentecostal literature in the previous six decades.

Pentecostals suffered disappointment when, on Christmas Day 1989, the Israeli Supreme Court denied Messianic Jews automatic citizenship under the 1950 Law of Return, saying that since they believe Jesus is the Messiah, they are Christians, not Jews.

In a happier tone, the *Pentecostal Evangel* reported the high drama associated with the massive secretive airlift known as Operation Solomon in May 1991. All Israel was charged with profound emotion as 14,087 Ethiopian Jewish people were airlifted in 36 hours to Israel. Also in 1992 the Bible Society in Israel stated that about 20 percent of Israeli homes had a New Testament.[72]

Messianic Jews struggled for their rights in Israel as more and more of them arrived from Eastern Europe and the former Soviet Union. That they found a champion was one piece of encouraging news. Rabbi Yitzhak Ralbag, chairman of the Jerusalem Religious Council, insisted that Messianic Jews were Jews indeed although they had "sinned in foolishness." He petitioned for civil rights for Israel's 3,000 Messianic Jews, but the 1989 Israel Supreme Court decision supported traditional prejudice and discouraged Messianic Jewish hope.

By 1998, the *Pentecostal Evangel* reported the Assemblies of God opposition to proposed Israeli legislation that would target Messianic Jews and deny them basic human rights. According to a press release from the Messianic Action Committee, the Israeli governing body was being asked to push Israel back into the darkest of the Middle Ages. The Assemblies of God sent thousands of dollars in support of that committee's resistance to ultra-orthodox efforts at heavy-handed religious persecution.[73]

The Pentecostal Evangel stood by its earlier declaration that "We believe the Jewish people are God's key to unlock the nations of the earth, God's explosive catalyst to set the world ablaze for Him.[74]

Epilogue

THE EVERLASTING BOND BETWEEN CLASSICAL PENTECOSTALISM AND THE JEWISH STATE

In the final analysis, in spite of the long-term political, theological, and sociological pressures to disassociate from national Israel, in addition to the two-decades-long confrontation with Muslim missionary issues, the Assemblies of God has not adopted a total hands-off policy toward Israel. A step in the direction of either Charismatic supersessionism or cessationist dispensationalism would undermine Pentecostalism's given reason for being. Some have attempted to redefine the proper use for speaking in tongues—classical Pentecostalism's strongest distinctive—and to disconnect Pentecostal restorationism from Zion's restoration. But any success of these efforts would only work to further undermine the given reason for classical Pentecostalism's existence as organizationally distinct from the Evangelical world.

No matter what position the Assemblies of God tended toward at different moments in the 20th century, it never felt at liberty to disavow Jewish evangelism. Since the Assemblies of God could not ignore the literal interpretation of Scripture, they felt obliged to take at face value the promises of Israel's ultimate restoration and salvation. This ultimate salvation of national Israel cannot be envisioned in Assemblies of God ideology as in any way divorced from Jewish national faith in Jesus Christ.

Earlier historians recognized the Protestant Reformation's departure from Roman Catholicism's Augustinian ideology of the role of Israel relative to the last days. This ultimately afforded Protestants a new significance for the Jewish people in space and time. Yet until now, no scholars have historically demonstrated the uniquely significant identification early Pentecostals made with the Jewish people, Zionism, and later with the State of Israel, as a correlative to the distinctive emphases made in 20th century Pentecostal ideology.

With the continued phenomenal numerical growth of Pentecostalism in North America and around the world, better understanding of Pentecostal history and ideology is of ever-increasing significance. In the light of its history, what might it mean in the 21st century?

ON A PERSONAL AND HEARTFELT NOTE

Students of Pentecostal ideological history need to awaken to the realities somehow observable between the historical lines found in this book. Behind the history of the relations between the chief Pentecostal denomination and "All Israel," one is able to catch a glimpse into the heart of God for His people, both Israel and the Church. Surely God has poured out His Spirit in great measure upon the last four and five generations of Pentecostals in anticipation of the Spirit-filled anointed followers of Jesus and Paul ultimately owning up to their responsibilities to brightly shine as the "signs, wonders, and miracles people" before Israel. Even as seen so many times in this history of Pentecostal ideology of Zion and the Jewish State, God has used the Spirit-filled tongues speakers to provide that "sign" the Jewish people somehow require to embrace the God-appointed Anointed One, Jesus. He is, after all, the One who is assigned by the Father to lead "all Israel" into her destiny.

Governing the world from Zion, Jesus, in His Second Coming, will enable Israel to perform her divine task of serving God and the nations He loves as "a kingdom of priests and a holy nation" (see 1 Pet. 2:9). Such a divine spiritual achievement among "All Israel" cannot be accomplished by the enticing words of man's wisdom, but in the power and demonstration of the Spirit of God. Wake up, O Pentecostal world, to your divine calling to bring "All Israel" to faith in this generation.

May it happen speedily and in our days!

GLOSSARY

Apostolic faith: The term American Pentecostals initially used to describe their movement as a last-days restoration of Christianity as practiced by the apostles in the first century.

Assemblies of God (AG): The designation of local churches affiliated with the General Council of the Assemblies of God.

Charismatic Renewal Movement (CRM): The movement penetrating non-Pentecostal historical denominations that has promoted the presence of the Spirit and spiritual giftedness.

Classical Pentecostals: Those members tracing their Pentecostal roots directly back to early 20th-century Pentecostalism.

Dispensationalism: The dividing of history into seven periods according to a perception of God's varied means of dealing with mankind in different eras.

Eschaton: The last days of time or the end of the age.

Glossolalia: Speaking in (sometimes ecstatic) tongues.

Holiness Movement: A large movement stemming out of Methodism in 19th-century American Christianity focused on personal perfection with special emphasis upon the works of the Holy Spirit.

Initial evidence: The doctrine that speaking in tongues is the mandatory evidence of the baptism in the Holy Spirit.

Latter Rain: With reference to prophecies in Joel 2:23 and Zechariah 10:1, early Pentecostals used the term latter rain to describe the 20th-century outpouring of the Holy Spirit.

Premillennialism: The view that Christ's second coming will happen before the one thousand years of utopian righteousness known as the Millennium.

Restorationism: The hope of bringing back 1st-century Christian practices. Restorationists tended to ignore history and based their teaching on the New Testament alone. Some early Pentecostals expected restoration of the apostolic power of New Testament Christianity immediately prior to the Second Coming.

COMMONLY USED ABBREVIATIONS:

AG: The General Council of the Assemblies of God

GPH: Gospel Publishing House, the AG publishing arm.

LRE: The Latter Rain Evangel

PE: The Pentecostal Evangel

ENDNOTES

FOREWORD

1. Leo, John, "When churches head left," *U.S. News and World Report,* Oct. 18, 2004.

2. Flame, "Twisted Words and Phrases (2). *U.S. News and World Report,* Oct. 18, 2004.

CHAPTER 1

1. Avihu Zakai, "The Poetics of History and the Destiny of Israel: the Role of the Jews in English Apocalyptic Thought during the Sixteenth and Seventeenth Centuries," *The Journal of Jewish Thought and Philosophy,* 5 (1996): 338-340.

2. Mason I. Lowance, Jr., *The Language of Canaan: Metaphor and Symbol in New England from the Puritans to the Transcendentalists* (Cambridge, MA: Harvard University Press, 1980), 161.

3. C. Leonard Allen, "Roger Williams and 'the Restauration of Zion'," *The American Quest for the Primitive Church*, ed. Richard T. Hughes (Urbana, IL: University of Illinois Press, 1988), 34.

4. Ibid., 35.

5. Peter Toon, ed., *Puritans, the Millennium and the Future of Israel: Puritan Eschatology 1600-1660* (Cambridge, UK: James Clarke, 1970), 71-72.

6. Catherine Albanese, *America, Religions, and Religion* (Boston, MA: Wadsworth/Cengage Learning, 2007), 117.

7. Reiner Smolinski, *"Israel Redivivus:* The Eschatological Limits of Puritan Typology in New England," *New England Quarterly* 63, no. 3 (September 1990): 364-365.

8. Ibid., 380-381.

9. Cotton Mather, "Problema Theologicum," 24, and Diary, 2:733. Quoted in Reiner Smolinski, *"Israel Redivivus,"* 385.

10. Nathan Hatch, *The Sacred Cause of Liberty* (New Haven, CT: Yale University Press, 1977), 28-30.

11. Albert C. Outler, "'Biblical Primitivism' in Early American Methodism," in *The American Quest for the Primitive Church*, ed. Richard T. Hughes (Urbana, IL: University of Illinois Press, 1988), 132-133.

12. Donald W. Dayton, *Theological Roots of Pentecostalism* (Peabody, MA: Hendrickson, 1987), 41.

13. Emory S. Bucke, ed., *History of American Methodism*, Vol. I (Nashville, TN: Abingdon Press, 1964), 298-301.

14. Dayton, *Theological Roots of Pentecostalism,* 150-151.

15. Hatch, *The Sacred Cause of Liberty*, 25-26.

16. Ibid., 48.

17. James W. Davidson, *The Logic of Millennial Thought* (New Haven, CT: Yale University Press, 1977), 116.

18. Paul Johnson, "The Almost-Chosen People," *First Things* 64 (2006): 82-83.

19. Ibid., 83.

20. Lowance, *The Language of Canaan*, 214-215.

21. Hatch, *The Sacred Cause of Liberty*, 52-53.

22. Ibid., 23-24.

23. Conor C. O'Brien, *God Land*, (Cambridge, MA: Harvard University Press, 1988), 29.

24. Hatch, *The Sacred Cause of Liberty*, 43-44.

25. Lowance, *The Language of Canaan*, 212-213.

26. Gershon Greenberg, *The Holy Land in American Religious Thought: 1620-1948* (Lanham, MD: University Press of America, 1994), 29-33.

27. Hatch, *The Sacred Cause of Liberty*, 21-22.

28. Paul Boyer, *When Time Shall Be No More* (Cambridge, MA: Belknap Press of Harvard University Press, 1992), 73-74.

29. Ibid., 181-183.

30. Dayton, *Theological Roots of Pentecostalism*, 153.

31. Jack P. Maddex, "Proslavery Millennialism," *American Quarterly* 31, no. I (Spring 1979): 47.

32. Boyer, *When Time Shall Be No More*, 90.

33. Albanese, *America, Religions, and Religion*, 189; 159-160.

34. Dayton, *Theological Roots of Pentecostalism*, 156-157.

35. Ibid.

36. Ibid., 72.

37. Edith Blumhofer, "Puritan and Preparation," *Reaching Beyond: Chapters in the History of Perfectionism*, Stanley Burgess, et al, eds. (Peabody, MA: Hendrickson, 1986), 263.

38. Maddex, "Proslavery Millennialism," 60.

39. Elizabeth Nottingham, *Methodism and the Frontier* (New York, NY: AMS Press, 1966), 194.

40. Franklin H. Littell, "The Power of the Restoration Vision and Its Decline in Modern America," *The Primitive Church in the Modern World*, ed. Richard T. Hughes (Urbana, IL: University of Illinois Press, 1995), 66.

41. Ibid., 124.

42. Clarence Bass, *Backgrounds to Dispensationalism* (Grand Rapids, MI: W.B. Eerdmans, 1960), 29.

43. Ibid., 29-30, 33.

44. Boyer, *When Time Shall Be No More*, 220.

45. Ibid., 89,226.

46. Edith Blumhofer, *Restoring the Faith: The Assemblies of God, Pentecostalism, and American Culture* (Urbana, IL: University of Illinois Press, 1993), 16.

47. Bass, *Backgrounds to Dispensationalism*, 100-101.

48. C. Norman Kraus, *Dispensationalism in America* (Richmond, VA: John Knox Press, 1958), 56, 126.

49. William E. Blackstone, *Jesus Is Coming* (Chicago, IL: F.H. Revell, 1908).

50. Ibid., 240.

51. Kraus, *Dispensationalism in America,* 72.

52. Ibid., 83, 91.

53. Dayton, *Theological Roots of Pentecostalism,* 163.

54. Earl Kennedy, "Prairie Premillennialism," *Reformed Review* (Winter 1992): 164.

55. Kraus, *Dispensationalism in America,* 104-105.

56. Blumhofer, *Restoring the Faith,* 29.

57. Kraus, *Dispensationalism in America,* 110,191.

58. Blumhofer, *Restoring the Faith,* 21.

59. Blumhofer, "Puritan and Preparation," 268-270.

60. Blumhofer, *Restoring the Faith,* 30-32.

61. Ibid., 31.

62. Albanese, *America, Religions, and Religion,* 172-173.

63. Blumhofer, "Puritan and Preparation," 267.

64. John Walsh, "'Methodism' and the Origins of English-Speaking Evangelicalism," *Evangelicalism,* Mark A. Noll, et al, eds. (New York, NY: Oxford University Press, 1994), 21.

65. Dayton, *Theological Roots of Pentecostalism,* 177.

66. R.A. Torrey, *The Baptism With the Holy Spirit* (New York, NY: Fleming H. Revell, 1897), 28.

67. W.H. Daniels, *Moody: His Words, Work, and Workers* (New York, NY: Nelson and Phillips, 1877), 396-399.

CHAPTER 2

1. Edith Blumhofer, *Restoring the Faith: The Assemblies of God, Pentecostalism, and American Culture* (Urbana, IL: University of Illinois Press, 1993), 11-12.

2. D. Wesley Myland, *The Latter Rain Covenant and Pentecostal Power* (Chicago, IL: Evangel Publishing House, 1910), viii-ix.

3. Robert Anderson, *Vision of the Disinherited* (Peabody, MA: Hendrickson, 1979), 224-225.

4. Ibid., 226.

5. J. Edwin Orr, *The Flaming Tongue* (Chicago, IL: Moody Press, 1973), 78.

6. Ibid, 226.

7. Ibid.

8. Vinson Synan, *The Holiness-Pentecostal Movement in the United States* (Grand Rapids, MI: Eerdmans, 1972), 177f.

9. Blumhofer, *Restoring the Faith*, 72.

10. Anderson, *Vision of the Disinherited*, 108-109.

11. Ibid., 107-108.

12. Charles F. Parham, *A Voice Crying in the Wilderness* (Baxter Springs, KS: Apostolic Faith Bible College, n.d., 2nd ed., 1910), 28.

13. Ibid., 27.

14. Paul K. Conkin, *American Originals: Homemade Varieties of Christianity* (Chapel Hill, NC: University of North Carolina Press, 1997), 295.

15. James S. Tinney, "William J. Seymour: Father of Modern Day Pentecostalism," in *Black Apostles,* eds. Randall Burkett and Richard Newman (Boston, MA: G.K. Hall and Co., 1978), 220.

16. Vinson Synan, *The Old-Time Power* (Franklin Springs, GA: Advocate Press, 1973), 105.

17. Conkin, *American Originals,* 299-300.

18. Orr, *The Flaming Tongue,* 185.

19. Blumhofer, *Restoring the Faith,* 107.

20. Alexander A. Boddy, "Seven Signs of His Coming," *Confidence* (December 1910): 281,288.

21. Margaret Poloma, *The Assemblies of God at the Crossroads* (Knoxville, TN: University of Tennessee, 1989), 37-38.

22. Grant Wacker, "Searching for Eden with a Satellite Dish: Primitivism, Pragmatism, and the Pentecostal Character," *The Primitive Church in the Modern World,* ed. Richard T. Hughes (Urbana, IL: University of Illinois Press, 1995), 142-3.

23. Ibid., 148.

24. Grant Wacker, "Playing for Keeps: The Primitivist Impulse in Early Pentecostalism," *The American Quest for the Primitive Church,* ed. Richard T. Hughes (Urbana, IL: University of Illinois Press, 1988), 210.

25. F.A. Bright, "Zionism," *Living Truths* 4:8 (August 1904): 462-465.

26. William MacArthur, "The Clock of Time," *Living Truths* 7:6 (June 1907): 317.

27. George Taylor, *The Spirit and the Bride* (Galcon, NC: Falcon Holiness School, 1907); reprint, Donald Dayton, ed., *Three Early Pentecostal Tracts* (New York, NY: Garland Publishing, 1985), 90-98.

28. Myland, *The Latter Rain Covenant*, 1.

29. Ibid., 3.

30. William Cossum, *Mountain Peaks of Prophecy and Sacred History* (Chicago, IL: Evangel Publishing Co., 1911): 68.

31. C. Antoszewski, "The City Shall Be Built From the Tower of Hananeel," *LRE* (1 March 1910): 11.

32. Eudorus N. Bell, "Preparations for the Return to Palestine," *Word and Witness* 12:8 (1 August 1915): 2.

33. "Next Year in Jerusalem," *LRE* (1 June 1917): 13.

34. Alice R. Flower, ed., "What Is Happening to Palestine?" *Weekly Evangel* (28 April 1917): 7.

35. "Next Year in Jerusalem," *LRE* (1 June 1917): 12-13.

36. Bernhard Angel, "The Jewish People and the Gospel," *Living Truths* 4:8 (August 1904): 469-473.

37. Louie Schneiderman, "Called to the Jewish People," *The Pentecost* 1:2 (September 1908): 2-3.

38. John G. Lake, "Latest News from Africa," *The Pentecost* 1:2 (September 1908): 2.

39. Joseph Lewek, "Bearing Persecution for Jesus' Sake," *LRE* (1 January 1912): 13-19.

40. A.A. Boddy, ed., "Jerusalem," *Confidence* 6:2 (February 1913): 40.

41. A.A. Boddy, "Sunderland Convention," *Confidence* 6 (June 1913): 114.

42. A.J. Benson, "God and the Jewish People," *Word and Witness* 9:6 (20 June 1913): 8.

43. Sarah Smith, "Jerusalem, Palestine," *Word and Witness* 9:8 (20 August 1913): 1.

44. "Fellowship in Christ," *Weekly Evangel* (11 August 1917).

45. Alberta Boothby, "Missionaries Back from Jerusalem," *Weekly Evangel* (3 March 1917): 13.

46. Phillip Sidersky, "I Am Only a Jew, But…" *Weekly Evangel* (11 August 1917): 11.

47. A.A. Boddy, "Transatlantic Experiences," *Confidence* 6:1 (January, 1913): 15.

48. Anderson, *Vision of the Disinherited,* 155-156.

49. Blumhofer, *Restoring the Faith,* 99, 84.

50. Ibid., 113-135.

CHAPTER 3

1. Edith Blumhofer, *Restoring the Faith: The Assemblies of God, Pentecostalism, and American Culture* (Urbana, IL: University of Illinois Press, 1993), 142-143.

2. Ibid., 137.

3. Ibid., 142.

4. Ibid., 159.

5. Vinson Synan, *The Holiness-Pentecostal Movement* (Grand Rapids, MI: Eerdmans, 1972), 205-206.

6. Ibid., 200-201.

7. Blumhofer, *Restoring the Faith*, 157-158.

8. Ibid., 149-150.

9. Ibid., 189.

10. "The Jewish People and Palestine," *Weekly Evangel* (5 January 1918): 5.

11. "Here and There," *PE* (13 September 1924): 8.

12. Frank Boyd, *The Budding Fig Tree* (Springfield, MO: GPH, 1925), 85-86; 97-99.

13. Myer Pearlman, "The Jewish Question From the Viewpoint of a Spiritually Redeemed Jew," *PE* (4 June 1927): 8.

14. Albert Weaver, "Chief Rabbi Kuk's Message to the Jewish People," *PE* (13 December 1930): 9.

15. Otto Klink, "The Jew—God's Great Timepiece," *PE* (15 May 1931): 5.

16. Myer Pearlman, "Shadow and Sunshine in Israel," *PE* (3 December 1932): 8.

17. "Jewish Notes," *PE* (13 December 1924): 6.

18. Charles Peters, "Eretz Israel," *PE* (2 April 1937): 5.

19. Charles Peters, "The Budding Fig Tree," *PE* (2 June 1934): 3.

20. "Rebuilding Palestine," *PE* (8 April 1944): 12.

21. H.C. McKinney, ed., "Prophetic News," *Word and Work* 55, no. 8 (August 1938): 5.

22. William Nagel, "Palestine—What of Its Progress," *PE* (7 November 1936): 10.

23. G. Murchie Jr., "Tide of New Age Floods Palestine," *LRE* (1 July 1934): 19-20.

24. Paul Rader, "Armageddon," *Confidence* 9:3 (July-September 1918): 43-45.

25. Alice Flower, "The Budding Fig Tree," *PE* (27 May 1922): 5.

26. Mark Levy, "A Son of Levi Writes to His Brethren," *PE* (24 November 1923): 23.

27. "Editor's Notes," *PE* (13 August 1927): 7.

28. Niels Thomsen, "The Present Jewish Crisis," *LRE* (1 June 1933): 15.

29. Frank Boyd, "The Budding Fig Tree," *PE* (7 July 1934): 6.

30. William Nagel, "Palestine—What of Its Progress," *PE* (31 October 1936): 8-9.

31. Myer Pearlman, "Daniel Speaks Today," *Christ's Ambassador's Herald* 15:2 (February 1942): 6.

32. Boyd, *The Budding Fig Tree*, 42-43.

33. GPH, "Lesson 11: God's Chosen People: the Jewish people," *Adult and Young People's Teacher's Quarterly* (10 December 1944): 59.

34. "Editor's Notebook," *PE* (1 August 1931): 4.

35. Charles Peters, "Ishmael and Isaac," *PE* (2 December 1933): 3.

36. GPH, "Lesson 10: Nehemiah Rebuilding the Wall of Jerusalem," *Adult and Young People's Teacher's Quarterly* (8 December 1935): 74.

37. "Perilous Times: Uprising in Palestine," *PE* (29 August 1936): 9.

38. "Here and There," *PE* (18 August 1923): 8.

39. "Editor's Notebook," *PE* (8 November 1930), 4; and (6 December 1930): 4.

40. E.F.M. Staudt, "Jerusalem, the Coming Center of the Nations," *PE* (28 April 1945): 3.

41. "A Forward Step of Faith," *LRE* (1 May 1919): 11.

42. Arthur Payne, "The Land of Promise," *PE* (5 April 1930): 4.

43. "Jewish Notes," *PE* (August 13, 1932): 3.

44. "The Abrahamic Blessing," *PE* (July 29, 1933): 7.

45. "The Cost of Anti-Semitism," *PE* (9 September 1939): 20.

46. A.A. Boddy, ed., "Jewish Notes," *Confidence* 124 (January-March 1921): 5.

47. Christine I. Peirce, "Looking From the Top," *PE* (16 April 1921): 7.

48. Myer Pearlman, *Through the Bible Book by Book* (Springfield MO: GPH, 1935) part I, 108; part II, 109-110.

49. Otto Klink, "Otto-Graphics," *CAH* 9:2 (February 1936): 16; and 9:5 (May 1936): 15.

50. E.S. Williams, "Be Encouraged, Ye Jewish people," *PE* (18 January 1941): 6.

51. Cited in Anderson, *Vision of the Disinherited*, 218.

52. S. Frodsham, ed., "The Budding Fig Tree," *PE* (15 April 1922): 1.

53. N.P. Thomsen, "Anglo-Israelism, Under the Searchlight of God's Word," *LRE* (1 May 1934): 3-6; Daniel Finestone, "Anglo-Israelism—Fact or Fancy?" *LRE* (1 May 1936): 13-15.

54. Nathan Beskin, "When the Antichrist Reigns," *LRE* (1 August 1931).

55. Meyer Pearlman, "Daniel Speaks Today," *CAH* 14:12 (December 1941): 11.

CHAPTER 4

1. Alexander Marks, "Our Debt to Israel," *PE* (16 August 1941): 3.

2. S.H. Frodsham, "Sunday School Lesson," *PE* (19 June 1937): 10.

3. Frank Boyd, "Israel and the Nations," *PE* (14 July 1934): 6.

4. "The Indigestible Jew," *PE* (17 June 1944): 3.

5. Pearlman, "Jewish Notes," *PE* (20 August 1932): 6.

6. Beskin, "The Truth About Their Protocols," 5.

7. E.B. Samuel, "Anti-Christian Propaganda Against the Jewish People," *PE* (18 and 25 May 1935): 1,9; 6,7.

8. Otto Klink, "Otto-Graphics," *CAH* 9:8 (August 1936).

9. John S. Conning, "Israel—What of Tomorrow?" *PE* (4 December 1943): 8.

10. "October 4—What Time Is It?" *CAH* 9:10 (October 1936): 15.

11. Charles Robinson, ed., "What Is the Proper Christian Attitude Toward the Jew?" *Christ's Ambassadors Monthly* 5:10 (October 1930): 15.

12. M. Glaser, "A Survey of Missions to the Jewish People in Continental Europe 1900-1950," (Ph.D. diss. Fuller School of World Mission and Institute of Church Growth, Fuller Theological Seminary, 1998), 159-161.

13. "The Editor's Notebook," *PE* (20 October 1945): 4-5.

14. Boyd, *The Budding Fig Tree*, 76,78,81-83, 111-114.

15. Max Reach, "The Mystery and Romance of Israel," *PE* (23 June 1945): 5.

16. E.N. Bell, "God's Grace to the Gentiles. And the Restoration of Israel," *Christian Evangel* (6 September 1919): 4.

17. "Protection for Palestine," *PE* (17 January 1942): 12.

18. Williams, "A New Day Coming to the Jewish People," 2.

19. Laura Radford, "God Fulfilling His Covenant with Abraham," *LRE* (1 February 1934): 3.

20. Frodsham, ed., "The Editor's Notebook," *PE* (28 May 1932): 5.

21. Boddy, "The Return of the Jewish people to the Holy Land, What it Portends," 55.

22. Frodsham, "The Coming Great Ingathering," *PE* (19 March 1938): 5.

23. "Jewish Notes," *PE* (25 April 1925): 7.

24. "Prophecies and Their Fulfillment in Palestine," *LRE* (1 June 1931): 1.

25. GPH, "Lesson 11: Jeremiah," *The Pentecostal Teacher's Quarterly* (14 September 1930): 92.

26. E.S. Williams, et al., "The Restoration of Israel," 30.

27. Ibid., 32.

28. "The Editor's Notebook," *PE* (30 April 1933): 4.

29. "When a Jew Met Jesus," 11.

30. "Here and There," *PE* (13 September 1924): 8.

31. "A Jewish Missionary," *PE* (6 September 1924): 7

32. "The Passing and the Permanent," *PE* (13 May, 1944): 16.

33. Aarmin Holzer, "From Synagogue to Pentecost," *LRE* (1 May 1925): 17-21.

34. Ruth Angel, "The Gospel in the Ghetto," *Christ's Ambassadors Monthly* 4, no. 5 (May 1929): 1,2,16.

35. M. Pearlman, "Jewish Notes," *PE* (27 July 1929): 5.

36. Pearlman, *Through the Bible Book by Book*, II, 89.

37. Pearlman, *The Synagogue of the Nazarenes* (Springfield, MO, GPH), 57-59.

38. Pearlman, "Those Strange People—The Jewish People!" 3.

39. GPH, "Lesson 11: God's Chosen People," *Adult and Young People's Teacher's Quarterly* (10 December 1944): 63.

40. Riggs, "The Jew," 2,12.

41. F. Bush, "Jerusalem, Palestine," *Christian Evangel* (10 October 1914): 4.

42. E. Brown, "Recent Conditions in Jerusalem," *LRE* (1 April 1918): 5.

43. William Faux, "Pentecost in Palestine," *PE* (12 September 1925): 11.

44. "In the Whitened Harvest Fields," *PE* (15 June 1929): 16.

45. Nathan C. Beskin, *Return of the Jews and the End of the World* (Chicago, IL: Peacock Press, 1931), 83, 140-141.

46. V. Swartzrauber, "Physical and Spiritual Transformation in Palestine," *LRE* (1 July 1935): 6,8.

47. "Editor's Notes," *PE* (11 October 1924): 9.

48. "Jewish Notes," *PE* (13 December 1924): 6-7.

49. "God's Wonderful Grace," *PE* (13 July 1929): 4.

50. Charles Spellman, "Jewish Evangelistic Work of California," *PE* (25 June 1921): 14.

51. Beskin, "The Return of the Jewish People," *LRE* (1 May 1931): 7.

52. Beskin, "The Truth About the Protocols," 21.

53 Meyer Tan Ditter, "Giving the Gospel to the Jewish People," *PE* (15 August 1936): 5.

54. Alexander Marks, "Evangelizing the Jewish People," *PE* (16 March 1940): 7.

55. "Council Jottings," *LRE* (1 October 1921): 11.

56. S. Frodsham, *With Signs Following* (Springfield, MO: GPH, 1926), 208-210.

57. Ibid., 211-212.

58. Ibid., 212-213.

59. Z. Arbue, "Despise Not Prophesyings," *Word and Work* 54:10 (October 1932): 4-5.

60. Frodsham, "Editor's Notebook," *PE* (30 April 1932): 4.

61. "Witnessing to Jewish People: Speaking Languages They Understand," *PE* (16 May 1942): 11.

62. Ibid.

CHAPTER 5

1. Margaret Poloma, *The Assemblies of God at the Crossroads* (Knoxville, TN: University of Tennessee, 1989), 239-240.

2. Ibid., 244.

3. See William Menzies, *Anointed to Serve* (Springfield, MO: GPH, 1971), 177-182.

4. By 1987 they represented over 60 percent of the combined five million NAE membership.

5. Richard Riss, *Latter Rain* (Mississauga, ON: Honeycomb Visual Productions Ltd., 1987), 11.

6. Blumhofer, *Restoring the Faith*, 243-244.

7. His earlier tendency to ideologically link the Church and Israel in the divine program was challenged by Boyd, Riggs, and Williams. Only Stanley Horton would provide the level of scholarship required to arrest the complete Assembly of God slide into dispensationalism.

8. Pearlman, *Knowing the Doctrines of the Bible*, 348-349.

9. Ralph Riggs, *The Bible's Backbone* (Springfield MO: GPH, 1945): 106-107.

10. Ibid., 116-117.

11. "Palestine, the Focal Spot of World Interest," *PE* (17 January 1948): 4,12-14.

12. Frodsham, "Man's Vain Attempts to Destroy Israel," *PE* (17 July 1948): 4-5.

13. "The Budding Fig Tree," *PE* (12 June 1948): 4.

14. Ibid., 124-125.

15. Hyman Apelman, "God Over Palestine," *PE* (14 May 1949): 6-7.

16. E.S. Williams, "Sunday School Lesson," *PE* (8 July 1950): 8.

17 "The Passing and the Permanent," *PE* (7 January 1950): 9.

18. "The Passing and the Permanent," *PE* (11 February 1950): 9.

19. "The Passing and the Permanent," *PE* (13 May 1950): 8.

20. "The Passing and the Permanent," *PE* (11 March 1950): 10.

21. Frank Boyd, "Israel's Glorious Future," *PE* (18 May 1952): 6-7.

22. Elmer Nicholas, "The Fig Tree Is Budding," *PE* (22 March 1953): 3-4.

23. E.S. Williams, *Systematic Theology*, Vol. 3 (Springfield, MO: GPH, 1953), 50,52,67.

24. Ralph Riggs, *We Believe* (Springfield, MO: GPH, 1954), 114.

25. Horton earned degrees from the University of California at Berkeley, Gordon-Conwell Theologicial Seminary, Harvard

University, and Central Baptist Theological Seminary. His teaching career began at Metropolitan Bible Institute in North Bergen, New Jersey (1945–48). He taught for 30 years at Central Bible College in Springfield, MO (1948–78). He went on to teach at the AG Theological seminary from 1978 until his retirement from active teaching in 1991. He also served from 1979 to 1980 as president of the Society for Pentecostal Studies. Upon leaving AGTS, he became the official coordinator of the Pentecostal Textbooks Project and general editor of Logion Press until his final retirement at age 84 in November 2000.

26. Stanley M. Horton, *Into All Truth* (Springfield MO: GPH, 1955), 86.

27. Ibid., 87.

28. Ibid., 108.

29. C.M. Ward, *Ishmael and Isaac* (Springfield MO: GPH, 1955), 6.

30. Ibid., 10.

31. Ibid., 11-12; 14-19,22.

32. C.M. Ward, "Will Israel Survive?" *PE* (14 October 1956): 6-7, 25.

33. Ibid.

34. Charles W.H. Scott, "World Crisis and Coming Events," *PE* (2 December 1956); 3,21-23.

35. Albert Hoy, "Israel's Message to the Church," *PE* (20 January 1957): 18-19.

36. "The Miracle of Israel," *PE* (November 1958): 2.

37. Cunningham, ed., "My Prayer for Israel," *PE* (21 February 1960): 2.

38. Cunningham, ed., "God's Plan for Palestine," *PE* (17 October 1965): 4.

39. Cunningham, ed., "Israel's 17th Birthday," *PE* (22 August 1965): 4.

40. C.M. Ward, "The Fountain," *Revivaltime Pulpit*, Number 10 (Springfield, MO: Assemblies of God National Radio Department, 1966): 164-165.

41. James Kimbrel, "Two Cities of Israel," *PE* (14 May 1967): 6-7.

42. Riggs, "Who is the Rightful Owner of Palestine?" *PE* (30 July 1967): 7.

43. Ward, "Israel's Temple Will Be Rebuilt," *Revivaltime Pulpit* Number 13 (Springfield, MO: AG National Radio Department, 1969): 289-290.

44. Ward, "And World Leaders Tremble," *PE* (18 May 1969): 14-15.

45. Frank Boyd, *The Spirit Works Today* (Springfield, MO: GPH, 1970): 71,78-80.

46. "Missions at Home," *PE* (21 September 1952).

47. Wallace Bragg, "Witnessing to the Jewish people in Philadelphia, *PT* (1 August 1954): 10-11.

48. Ruth Specter, "Are We Doing Our Duty?" *PE* (28 July 1957): 3,21.

49. Nate Scharff, "Jewish people Don't Know Who Christ Is," *PE* (20 March 1960): 20-21.

50. Ruth Toczek, "The Jewish Nation—Yesterday and Today," *PE* (24 September 1961): 5.

51. Ernest Kalapathy, "Israel's Hope," *PE* (25 July 1965): 22-23.

52. E. Kalapathy, "Why Jewish People Need the Gospel," *PE* (31 March 1968): 21.

53. "Interest High in Second Jewish Evangelism Seminar," *PE* (25 April 1971): 22-23.

CHAPTER 6

1. Grant Wacker, "Searching for Eden," *The Primitive Church in the Modern World*, ed. Richard T. Hughes (Urbana, IL: University of Illinois Press, 1995), 140.

2. Blumhofer, *Restoring the Faith*, 253-254.

3. Ibid., 260.

4. C.M. Ward, "Pray for the Peace of Jerusalem," *PE* (23 January 1975): 8.

5. C.M. Ward, "A Burdensome Stone for All People," *PE* (13 November 1977): 20-21.

6. Paul Boyer, *When Time Shall Be No More* (Cambridge, MA: Harvard University Press, 1992), 203.

7. Danny Collum, "Armageddon Theology as a Threat to Peace," *Faith and Mission* (Fall 1986): 60.

8. L.V.D. Tiller, "What Is God Doing in Israel?" *PE* (10 February 1975): 8-9.

9. C.M. Ward, "Pray for the Peace of Jerusalem," *PE* (26 January 1975): 9.

10. Ibid.

11. Hal Lindsey, *The Late Great Planet Earth* (Grand Rapids, MI: Zondervan, 1971).

12. David Wilkerson, *The Vision* (Old Tappan, NJ: Fleming H. Revell, 1974), 98-99.

13. C.M. Ward, "Israel Will Survive," *PE* (8 June 1975): 22.

14. George E. Ladd, *The Last Things* (Grand Rapids, MI: Eerdmans, 1978), 27.

15. Boyer, *When Time Shall Be No More*, 273.

16. Stanley Horton, *What You Should Know About Prophecy* (Springfield MO: GPH, 1975), 99,101,105.

17. C.M. Ward, "All Israel Shall be Saved," *Revivaltime Pulpit: Sermon Book 20* (Springfield, MO: AG National Radio Department, 1976), 232-237.

18. Vinson Synan, "The Role of Tongues as Initial Evidence," paper presented to the Society for Pentecostal Studies (11-13 November 1993), 5,12.

19. Luther Gerlach, "Pentecostalism" in Religious Movements in Contemporary America, eds. I. Zaretsky and M. Leone (Princeton, NJ: Princeton University Press, 1974), 675-676.

20. Ibid., 684-685.

21. Derek Prince, *The Last Word on the Middle East* (Lincoln, VA: Chosen Books, 1982).

22. M. Unger, *Beyond the Crystal Ball* (Chicago, IL: Moody Press, 1973), 108.

23. Peter Stiglin, "Apocalyptic Theology and the Right," *Witness* (October 1986): 9.

24. Hal Lindsey, *The 1980s: Countdown to Armageddon* (Toronto: Bantam, 1982), 176.

25. Tim LaHaye, *The Coming Peace in the Middle East* (Grand Rapids, MI: Zondervan, 1984), 63.

26. Boyer, *When Time Shall Be No More*, 206.

27. Horton, "I Will Put MY Spirit Within You," *Paraclete* 11:2 (Spring 1977): 9.

28. Ibid., 10-11.

29. Amos Millard, "The Holy Spirit and the Restoration of Israel," *Paraclete* 12:2 (Spring 1978): 6-7; 9-10.

30. Y. Ariel, *Evangelizing the Chosen People* (Chapel Hill, NC: University of North Carolina Press, 2000), 202.

31. Ruth Lyon, "A New Look at Jewish Ministry," *PE* (30 December 1973): 21.

32. E. Kalapathy, "The Jewish people and Jesus," *PE* (16 September 1973): 21.

33. Ruth Lyon, "Baruch Ha-Shem! It's Happening!" *PE* (11 January 1976): 19.

34. Melanie Burg, "He is Among Us," *PE* (26 March 1978): 14.

35. "We are Reaching American Jewish People," *PE* (31 July 1983): 18-19.

36. Carole Nelson, "Light Unto the Nations," *PE* (26 July 1981): 15.

37. David Lewis, *Magog 1982, Cancelled* (Harrison, AR: New Leaf Press, 1982), 44.

38. Grant Jeffrey, *Armageddon,* (New York, NY: Bantam, 1990), 105-106.

39. Naisbitt and Aburcense, *Megatrends 2000* (New York, NY: William Morrow, 1990), 270,

40. Poloma, *The Assemblies of God at the Crossroads* (Knoxville, TN: University of Tennessee, 1989), 208-209; 240-241.

41. "Outbreak of Anti-Semitism Reported in U.S.," *PE* (14 June 1981): 24.

42. Mark Hanna, "Israel Today" *Christianity Today* 26 (22 January 1982): 15-17.

43. J. Van Impe, *Israel's Final Holocaust* (Nashville, TN: T. Nelson, 1979), 77.

44. D. Wilson, "Pentecostal Perspectives on Eschatology," *Dictionary of Pentecostal and Charismatic Movements,* eds., Burgess, McGee, Alexander (Grand Rapids, MI: Regency Reference Library, 1988).

45. "Emigration Concerns Israel Government," *PE* (20 December 1981): 21

46. D.R. Wilkerson, *Set the Trumpet to Thy Mouth* (Lindale, TX: World Challenge, Inc., 1985), 11.

47. Dan Betzer, *The Most Dangerous Man in the World* (Springfield, MO: GPH 1981), 21.

48. "Assembly of God Evangelist Shares in Historic Gathering," *PE* (5 July 1981): 13.

49. David A. Rausch, "Chosen People: Christian Views of Judaism are Changing," *Christianity Today* 32 (7 October 1988): 58-59.

50. David Chilton, *Paradise Restored* (Tyler, TX: Reconstruction Press, 1985), 224.

51. David Chilton, *The Days of Vengeance* (Fort Worth, TX: Dominion Press, 1987), 127-128; 618-619.

52. Grant Wacker, "Playing for Keeps," *The American Quest for the Primitive Church*, ed. Richard T. Hughes (Urbana, IL: University of Illinois Press, 1988), 215.

53. A. Millard, "The Prophecy of Joel," *Paraclete* 17:2 (Spring 1983): 12.

54. Timothy P. Weber, "Happily at the Edge of the Abyss: Popular Premillennialism in America," *Ex Auditu* 6 (1990): 90.

55. S.M. Horton, *Our Destiny* (Springfield, MO: Logion Press, 1996), 177.

56. Grant McClung, "Mission in the 1990s: Three Views," *International Bulletin of Missiological Research* 14:4 (1 October 1990): 153.

57. James K.A. Smith, "The Closing of the Book," *Journal of Pentecostal Theology* 11 (1997): 70-71.

58. Gordon Anderson, "Pentecostal Hermeneutics," Part II, *Paraclete* 28:2 (Spring 1994): 17.

59. Horton, *Our Destiny*, 191-194.

60. Ibid., 196-197.

61. Ralph Harris, "Thank God for the Jewish People," *PE* (23 December 1994): 22.

62. J.R. Church, "The Nation of Israel," *The Trimphant Return of Christ*, David Breese, et al (Green Forest, AR: New Leaf Press, 1993), 263, 278-279.

63. Dwight Wilson, "Pentecostal Perspectives on Eschatology," *Dictionary of Pentecostal and Charismatic Movements*.

64. Ariel, "American Fundamentalists and the Emergence of a Jewish State," 302,308.

65. David Lewis, *New 95 Theses* (Springfield, MO: Menorah Press, 1995), 5.

66. Grant Jeffrey, *Prince of Darkness* (Toronto, ON: Frontier Research Publications, 1994), 126-127.

67. William Menzies and Stanley Horton, *Bible Doctrines* (Springfield, MO: Logion Press, 1993), 236,238.

68. S. Horton, ed., *Systematic Theology* (Springfield, MO: Logion Press, 1994), 621-622.

69. Ibid., 630.

70. Horton, *Our Destiny*, 210.

71. These were the 3 July 1977 and 7 January 1979 lessons in the ATQ.

72. "Bible Society in Israel Prints Pocket-sized New Testament," *PE* (23 February 1992): 24.

73. "A/G Denounces Proposed Antimissionary Legislation," *PE* (2 April 1998): 23.

74. Daniel Gruber, "Speaking the Truth in Love," *PE* (18 November 1990): 21.

ABOUT THE AUTHOR

Dr. Raymond L. Gannon is currently serving as Visiting Professor of Missions and Jewish Studies at Assemblies of God Theological Seminary (Springfield, MO) and Director of Messianic Jewish Studies at The King's University (Van Nuys, CA). He has earned multiple graduate degrees at the California Graduate School of Theology (M.A., Ph.D.); Assemblies of God Theological Seminary (M.A., M.Div.); Princeton Theological Seminary (Th.M.); and The Hebrew University of Jerusalem (Ph.D.). Dr. Gannon has trained missionaries and pastors for over 30 years; he has served as a pastor of three A/G Messianic Jewish congregations and has been heavily involved in founding and developing Jewish ministries in Israel and in the United States. As a professor of History, Missions, and Jewish Studies, Dr. Gannon has taught at many institutions in the United States and abroad, including Central Bible College, Assemblies of God Theological Seminary, and Israel College of the Bible. He has published extensively on Jewish and Pentecostal topics, and he is currently acting as a translator and theologian for the Tree of Life Bible project. Dr. Gannon and his wife of 43 years, Kassiani S. Gannon, have three adult children and eleven grandchildren.

FOR MORE INFORMATION, CONTACT:

Address: P.O. Box 2389, Springfield, MO 65801-2389

Phone: (602) 288 5422

Email: RayGannon@TheKingsJewishVoice.org

In the right hands, This Book will Change Lives!

Most of the people who need this message will not be looking for this book. To change their lives, you need to put a copy of this book in their hands.

> *But others (seeds) fell into good ground, and brought forth fruit, some a hundred-fold, some sixty-fold, some thirty-fold* (Matthew 13:8).

Our ministry is constantly seeking methods to find the good ground, the people who need this anointed message to change their lives. Will you help us reach these people?

> *Remember this—a farmer who plants only a few seeds will get a small crop. But the one who plants generously will get a generous crop* (2 Corinthians 9:6).

EXTEND THIS MINISTRY BY SOWING
3 BOOKS, 5 BOOKS, 10 BOOKS, **OR MORE TODAY,**
AND BECOME A LIFE CHANGER!

Thank you,

Don Nori Sr., Founder
Destiny Image
Since 1982

DESTINY IMAGE PUBLISHERS, INC.

"Promoting Inspired Lives."

VISIT OUR NEW SITE HOME AT
WWW.DESTINYIMAGE.COM

FREE SUBSCRIPTION TO DI NEWSLETTER

Receive free unpublished articles by top DI authors, exclusive discounts, and free downloads from our best and newest books.

Visit www.destinyimage.com to subscribe.

Write to: Destiny Image
P.O. Box 310
Shippensburg, PA 17257-0310

Call: 1-800-722-6774

Email: orders@destinyimage.com

For a complete list of our titles or to place an order
online, visit www.destinyimage.com.

FIND US ON FACEBOOK OR FOLLOW US ON TWITTER.

www.facebook.com/destinyimage   facebook
www.twitter.com/destinyimage   twitter